NEW TESTAMENT GUIDES

General Editor
A.T. Lincoln

MATTHEW

MATTHEW

John Riches

Sheffield Academic Press

Copyright © 1996 Sheffield Academic Press

Published by Sheffield Academic Press Ltd
Mansion House
19 Kingfield Road
Sheffield, S11 9AS
England

Printed on acid-free paper in Great Britain
by The Cromwell Press
Melksham, Wiltshire

British Library Cataloguing in Publication Data

A catalogue record for this book is available
from the British Library

ISBN 1-85075-741-0

Contents

Contents

1

LEADING QUESTIONS IN MATTHAEAN SCHOLARSHIP

Introduction

The discipline of New Testament studies has its perennial questions and methods of answering them; it also undergoes changes of mood and interest when the focus of scholars' attention shifts from one set of issues to another, when certain methods and approaches gain favour. A study guide of this kind should, I think, both try to indicate something of the questions and ways of tackling them which have engaged Matthaean scholars over the years and also to give at least a flavour of the current debates which animate scholars working in the field.

When Donald Senior wrote his excellent guide to recent Matthaean scholarship in the early 1980s (*What Are They Saying about Matthew?* [New York: Paulist Press, 1983]), he focused first on questions of the setting, sources and structure of Matthew's Gospel and then turned for the bulk of his survey to questions of Matthew's theology: his views on salvation history, the Old Testament, the Law, christology, the church. That is to say his book reflects accurately the concern of scholars of the 60s and 70s to chart as fully as possible the evangelist's own theological stance. They wanted to discover the view of the Christian faith and practice that Matthew was trying to advocate as he edited his sources and presented them in the form of a Gospel like, but significantly different from, Mark's.

If one were to write the same kind of survey today one

would certainly want to focus it rather differently. Of course, there has not been a total sea-change over the last ten years. But, on the one hand, there has been greater interest in the community out of which Matthew came and for which he wrote, on the ways in which his contemporaries might have read and received his Gospel, and indeed on the ways in which it has been received in the churches subsequently. On the other hand, there has also been a change in the ways in which Matthew's own work is viewed. If earlier scholarship focused on the way in which Matthew took up and made detailed modifications to his sources, more recent studies have been interested in the way in which Matthew composed his narrative, in the overall shape which he gave to his work. This kind of interest also goes hand in hand with a renewed discussion about the sort of literature which Gospels are, indeed with a renewed interest in the biblical writings as literature, rather than as historical sources for the views and practice of the early church.

The nature of such shifts in scholarship can be exaggerated. Obviously scholars cannot keep on going over the same ground endlessly and so there are bound to be shifts of emphasis and fashion. However, some claims need to be treated with a little caution, for example, that the new literary approaches to the Bible have broken the mould of biblical studies. On the other hand, it is important to note where there is change in scholarly consensus in a discipline, just as it is important that there should be such changes. A discipline which never changed its mind would be one which was stagnant. Equally a discipline which never entertained new ways of looking at its subject matter or which was never prepared to learn from developments in other cognate areas of study would also be in danger of ossification.

So we shall follow a simple path in this guide. The first chapter will take a look at the major questions which have engaged scholars over the years, and at the ways in which they have tried to answer them. This will at least serve to map out the territory.

Then we shall proceed more selectively under three main heads. First, we shall consider questions of the literary form and nature of the Gospel, its sources, its relation to other literary forms, its structure and composition, and the new literary modes of reading the Gospel. Next we shall look at Matthew's community, its place in the development of the early church, its relation to other forms of religious belief, its internal dynamics and problems, and briefly, its subsequent reception in the church. This will provide a spring-board for considering the evangelist's own theology, specifically his christology. Here we shall consider how his theology is expressed through his use of a narrative form, as well as through his careful modification of the texts which he has taken over. This choice of topics will make it possible to give an idea of how the discipline has developed over the last ten years or more and to place recent contributions to the debate in the framework of perennial questions which have intrigued scholars in this field of studies.

Obviously what I choose to highlight would not be everyone's choice. This kind of book can make no claim to comprehensiveness. I would hope, however, that it will help most of its readers to read Matthew with more enjoyment and understanding than previously, and that it will encourage many to make good my deficiencies by reading their way more fully into some of the scholarly discussions themselves.

Data Concerning the Gospel of Matthew

What then are the questions which have engaged scholars working on Matthew's Gospel over the years? Perhaps the easiest way to answer this question is to set out some of the raw data concerning the Gospel itself, and then to see how the main questions arise out of the conjunction of certain aims and interests on the part of the interpreters with the matter on which they are working.

The first and most obvious thing to say about Matthew's Gospel is that it is one of three very similar works of literature in the New Testament. That is to say, it is very like Mark and Luke in form, content and indeed phrasing, and rather less like John, particularly as regards content and phrasing.

When the first three Gospels (known as the Synoptic Gospels) are set out side by side certain things become immediately apparent. In the first place they all follow to a considerable degree a common order. Certainly there are significant differences, not least in the way the teaching material is arranged in Matthew and Luke, but the agreement between the three is so significant as to require some kind of explanation. Secondly, it becomes apparent that there are remarkable agreements in the way the stories and sayings are narrated in all three Gospels. This is not just a matter of agreement about what actually happened or about the substance of what was said, such as one might expect from faithful and intelligent eye-witnesses. It is rather a matter of word for word agreement in the way the incidents and sayings are recorded, which suggests some dependence on a common source, oral or literary.

Let us consider the nature of these agreements a little further, particularly as they relate to Matthew. Matthew has all but about 50 of Mark's 662 verses. There is also substantial agreement between Matthew and Mark in the order in which stories and sayings are presented, particularly in the second half of Matthew's Gospel. Additionally, Matthew has some 230 verses in common with Luke, most of which contain sayings of Jesus. However the order in which these sayings occur in Matthew and Luke is for the most part quite different. As well as these two very substantial bodies of material, about a quarter of Matthew is not found in either of the two other Synoptic Gospels. As we shall see, all of this will generate some intriguing discussions about the relationships between the Gospels and about the source of Matthew's material.

This measure of agreement between the first three Gospels makes it possible to see why it is necessary to distinguish the first three Gospels from the fourth. Nothing like the same agreement in order or in content occurs between any of the first three and John. There are moreover substantial differences in the accounts they offer of Jesus' ministry and teaching. In the Synoptics, Jesus conducts his ministry in the north of the country before going up to Jerusalem to die. In the Fourth Gospel he moves back and forth between Galilee and Jerusalem. There are interesting disagreements too about the details of the story: in John, the 'cleansing' of the

Temple occurs at the beginning of the Gospel; Jesus' ministry starts before John is put in prison; Jesus performs no exorcisms; Jesus' arrest is precipitated by the raising of Lazarus (not recorded in the Synoptics); the date of the crucifixion is different (in John it coincides with the slaughter of the Passover lambs, in the Synoptics it is on the day before). Perhaps more significant than this are two other facts. First, we need to note that where there is common material between the synoptics and the Fourth Gospel, as for example with the story of the centurion (Mt. 8.5-13; Lk. 7.1-10; Jn 4.46-53), there is often such a difference in the details of the telling of the story that we cannot easily suppose they knew each other's account. Secondly, there is a world of difference between the kind of teaching that is ascribed to Jesus in the Synoptic Gospels and in John. In the Synoptics, Jesus for the most part utters short sayings: proverbs, legal and prophetic sayings, parables, etc. Sometimes these occur, as in Matthew, in longer discourses, but even here the discourses are composed of a number of shorter sayings. By contrast Jesus' teaching in John is typically given in long discourses which focus significantly on questions about his own person and make explicit claims about his divine mission and nature which it is hard to parallel in the Synoptics. In this respect the saying in Mt. 11.27 is exceptional and is sometimes referred to as the 'Johannine thunderbolt'.

In short, we may say that Matthew's Gospel forms one of a group of three which are marked out by their very close agreements in order and detailed phraseology; that they share a common pattern for Jesus' ministry and agree significantly both in the kinds of activity which they ascribe to him: preaching, teaching, healing and exorcism and in the kind of teaching which he is portrayed as giving: very broadly of a kind for which it is not difficult to find formal parallels in the contemporary Jewish world.

However, while it is important to begin by emphasizing these shared characteristics, there are, of course, significant differences between Matthew and the other Synoptics which can best be sketched by giving a brief account of the contents of Matthew's Gospel and drawing attention within it to certain specific features of his work.

The content of Matthew's Gospel can conveniently be set out and memorized in a small diagram:

1–2	Genealogy and infancy narratives
3–4	John the Baptist and the beginnings of Jesus' ministry
5–7	The Sermon on the Mount
8–9	The miracles of Jesus
10	The Mission Discourse
11–12	John the Baptist and controversies over Jesus' miracles
13	Jesus' parables
14–17	Death of John; first feeding and walking on the lake; discussion of purity; Canaanite woman; second feeding miracle; discussion of miracles; Peter's confession; discipleship sayings; Transfiguration; faith and miracles; Temple tax.
18	Community rule
19–22	Teaching on divorce, celibacy; the commandments; wealth; the parable of the Labourers in the Vineyard; greatest in the kingdom; healing of the blindmen; triumphal entry and cleansing of the Temple; fig tree and teaching in Jerusalem
23	Woes on the Pharisees
24–25	Apocalyptic discourse
26–28	Passion and Resurrection

We shall discuss Matthew's way of composing and the relationships between his Gospel and the others more fully in the next chapter. Here we simply need to make a number of preliminary observations. First, unlike Mark but like Luke, Matthew starts his Gospel with stories about the young Jesus. Secondly, there are a number of major discourses positioned fairly regularly through the Gospel. Not all the teaching material is found here but these five blocks (5–7; 10; 13; 18; 24–25) are striking features of the Gospel, not found in the same measure in Mark or Luke. Thirdly, from ch. 14 onwards it becomes less easy to give neat summaries of the non-discourse chapters. This is most easily explained by saying that Matthew is here following Mark. Certainly he is closest to Mark in these sections.

So much for the bare outlines of Matthew's Gospel. It

will be useful here also to list some of the more specific characteristics of Matthew's material.

1. Matthew has ten quotations from the Old Testament which are typically introduced by a formula of the form: 'to fulfil what the Lord declared through the prophet': Mt. 1.22-23; 2.15,17-18, 23; 4.14-16; 8.17; 12.17-21; 13.35; 21.4-5; 27.9-10.

2. Matthew uses a range of titles for Jesus: Lord, Son of David, Son of Man, Son of God, Son, Christ, King of the Jews. Some of these titles occur more frequently than in Mark.

3. A number of traits in Matthew's story indicate a strong sense of separation between Matthew's community and the people of Israel: references to 'their synagogues' (12.9, cf. Mk 3.1; 13. 54, cf. Mk 6.2); statements to the effect that the Kingdom has been taken away from the Pharisees and High Priests (Mt. 21.43, cf. 22.1-14); the crowd's calling down Jesus' blood on themselves and their descendants (27.25); Jesus' sending his disciples to the Gentiles after his resurrection (Mt. 28.18-20).

4. Nevertheless, Matthew has a strong interest in the Law as is evidenced by his grouping of Jesus' teaching into the Sermon on the Mount and by the sayings strongly affirmative of the Law in that complex (5.17-20, esp. 5.18). At the same time, however, Matthew underlines the difference between the traditional teaching of Israel and Jesus' teaching by the 'antitheses' in the Sermon on the Mount (statements of the form 'You have heard it said...but I say unto you': 5.21-22, 27-28, 31-32, 33-34, 38-39, 43-44).

5. Matthew is the only evangelist who refers to the 'church' (ἐκκλησία): 16.18; 18.17.

Clearly, the 'raw data' which I have just set down are themselves matters to which scholars working on Matthew's Gospel have drawn attention over the years. How people see and read the Gospel depends a great deal on their particular viewpoint. Nevertheless, those data do represent some of the clearly statable facts about the Gospel which are worth mem-

orizing and which will provide the basis for our coming
discussions.

What sorts of enquiry are raised in scholars' minds by such
data? The answer to that question depends to a considerable
degree on the state of the scholars' minds themselves, more
particularly on the beliefs and aims with which they
approach the texts. One of the fascinating things about New
Testament studies is that scholars who are engaged in them
do indeed represent a great variety of viewpoints and are
often pursuing very different goals and agenda.

Some will see the canonical texts as together constituting
divine revelation and will therefore principally be concerned
to understand the ways in which Matthew's Gospel contributes to the content or purport of that revelation.

The facts about the relationships between the Gospels
which we have noted will raise some quite thorny questions
in this regard. The more clearly it is appreciated that
Matthew's Gospel was written by taking and *adapting* other
written sources, including Mark, the more difficult it will be
simply to harmonize the Gospel accounts. Biblical theologians working on the Gospels need to provide a positive
explanation of the diversity of Gospel accounts of Jesus' life,
teaching, death, passion and resurrection.

One way of providing such an explanation that has been
extremely attractive to many theologians over the last 30
years is through what is known as redaction critical studies.
If Matthew's Gospel is the result of his drawing together
different literary sources and editing them in such a way
that they form a composite whole, then it will be interesting
to look in detail at the ways in which he has edited those
sources. Careful scrutiny of the fine editorial touches he
made to the texts he took over will provide us with clues to
the particular perspective from which he views his story.
So too will an examination of the overall structure and
composition of his Gospel (sometimes referred to as 'composition criticism'). In these ways we may hope to arrive at a
theology of Matthew which can be set alongside that of Mark
and Luke.

What such studies show above all are the analogies
between Matthew's modes of working and those of other

literary editors. It shows him, that is to say, as a human author reflecting on the story which he has received. He is not simply a recorder of divine–human history: his reflections on that history are part of the process by which its meaning and message are made known. The theologies of Matthew, Mark and Luke are part of a tradition of biblical theologizing which continues on into the history of biblical interpretation in the church.

Others may be more interested in the history of the ancient world and of the Christian community in particular. They will want to know as much as they can about the development of early Christianity and its relation to other religious movements in the ancient world. Their reasons for this may be various. They may see the hand of divine providence in such movements and wish to understand the way in which they contribute to the 'education of humankind'. They may alternatively recognize that such movements have played and indeed continue to play an important part in the life of human society and wish to contribute to the better understanding of such powerful contemporary forces. They may simply enjoy uncovering the past.

Again the particular character of Matthew's Gospel will raise interesting questions for those of such an historical bent. The placing of Matthew within a particular stratum of Christian history, the Synoptic tradition, is itself an important lead for those trying to write a history of the development of the early Christian communities. At the same time the references within the Gospel to the Jewish community and to the Law draw our attention to the Matthaean community's relation to Judaism, which was itself undergoing major restructuring at this point in the wake of the destruction of the Temple in 70 CE. There are fascinating and extraordinarily complicated questions to be addressed here about the lines of development within the Judaeo-Christian tradition. In what sense does Christianity emerge out of the Jewish tradition? To what extent are post-70 Judaism and Christianity both off-shoots of pre-70 Judaism? And at the same time there are questions to be asked about the development of the human moral and religious consciousness. Should Matthew's digest of Jesus' teaching be described as a 'new law'? Does the teaching of the Sermon on the Mount stand as a major and largely innovative contribution to the development of human moral consciousness? Or indeed, more darkly, what is Matthew's contribution to the growth of anti-Semitism in Europe? What is his contribution to the development of exclusivist understandings of the church?

Yet again others may be interested in the biblical texts as works of literature. It is not so much what their authors once intended to say which intrigues such scholars as the varieties of ways in which such *texts* may convey meaning. Texts, that is to say, are not simply messages sent by an author to a particular destination; they are literary entities which have the power to convey meanings even when they have become divorced in time from their original context. They have the power to shape communities, indeed to create new worlds of meaning which may again lead to new readings of the texts.

Those who approach Matthew from such a broad standpoint are not always interested in the sort of data about literary sources and relationships that were discussed above. They may regard Matthew's relation to the Synoptic tradition and to Mark as being largely irrelevant to questions of the literary character of Matthew's Gospel as such. A 'purely' literary study of Matthew would consider the work as it stands and explore, for example, the Gospel's narrative character, employing a range of concepts drawn from modern literary theory. Others may be interested in the ways in which readers of the Gospel receive it and again may consider the literary history prior to the final form of the text irrelevant to such an undertaking. For them the text is constituted less by its relations to its antecedents than by its relation to those who read and make of it what they, and their interpretive communities, will.

On the other hand, those who wish to know more about the literary character of the text may find much to help them in the presentation of data above. It will help them in the task of understanding the literary process of production, just as it will be of help in the task of determining the literary character of the New Testament texts in relation to the other literary genres of the time. It will be grist to the mill of those

who wish to situate the Gospels in a literary history which
stretches from the earliest Gospel to the most recent
commentary on Matthew.

Such questions—theological, historical and literary—are
not hermetically sealed off from each other. Questions don't
put themselves, they are put by real people who have a
variety of interests and may each participate in a number of
different communities which variously pursue different
enquiries and conversations. In what follows we shall therefore not simply divide the book up under these three heads of
enquiry. Even though each chapter will take up a subject
which seems to fit neatly under one of these headings, in
practice each chapter will raise historical, literary and theological questions. In Chapter 2 we shall consider the literary
origins, character and history of the first Gospel. Here the
enquiry is principally literary and historical, but theological
matters will not be far afield. A literary and historical view of
the biblical writings raises sharp enough questions about the
way in which truth is conveyed through the Gospels. We
shall see how the nature of the enquiry changes from the
early interest in literary sources, to a focus on the largely
oral tradition behind the Gospels and then on again to
the question of their literary form and of the authorial
activity of the Evangelists. Finally, we shall look at some
more recent contributions which threaten to leave the
historical dimension behind altogether and instead focus
attention exclusively on the literary, narrative character of
the Gospel.

In Chapter 3 we shall turn to matters more strictly
historical: the location of Matthew's community in the
development of early Christianity and Judaism and the
subsequent history of the reception of Matthew's Gospel in
the church. But here again literary and theological matters
will also play an important part. The question of literary
origins and subsequent literary history will help us to get a
fix on Matthew's community. And so too will questions of
theology. The more we know about the theological positions
adopted by Matthew, the easier it will be to situate
him among the diverse forms of early Christian and Jewish
belief; the more we know about the subsequent theological

exploitation of Matthew's text, the more we shall know about its potential for meaning.

Finally, in Chapter 4 we shall look at a specifically theological topic: Matthew's christology. Interestingly, we shall see here how different views of the literary structure and character of the Gospel affect scholars' views of the content of Matthew's Gospel. We shall see how Matthew's theological ideas are expressed not only in the titles which he gives to Jesus, but also in the way those titles are placed in the Gospel, the way they are elaborated by association with other texts and figures from the Old Testament and by the narrative in which they are found. And of course the more we understand about the setting in which Matthew is writing, the more we shall understand about this process of elaboration.

2

WHAT SORT OF A BOOK?

THIS CHAPTER WILL DEAL with literary matters: how was Matthew written, what sort of a book was it, where do we place such literature in the ancient world, what modes of reading are appropriate to this kind of work of literature?

Such questions have often been dealt with in Introductions to the New Testament, almost as a separate branch of the subject. There is something to be said for this: similar questions arise about other books and it is convenient to lump such discussions together. Much of what we say here will be, with suitable modifications, applicable to other Gospels. Nevertheless, too sharp a separation of such questions from detailed interpretation of the text is inadvisable. Views about the literary sources, genre and structure of Matthew will need to be tested against a close reading of the Gospel itself.

These are important preliminary questions. It makes a difference to the way we read something whether it is an anthology, a monograph, a novel, a letter, a set of essays, a dissertation. At least it does if we are aware of its literary nature. It helps us to know how to relate the parts to the whole, how to identify the author's own emphases and comments.

Sources

Discussions about the sources of the Synoptic Gospels are for some people all absorbing, for others rather arcane crossword puzzles which seem of little importance to the central task of interpreting the Gospels. One may not want to devote one's life to solving the problem, but in order to understand the study of Matthew it is at least essential to see what the problem is.

Put at its simplest the problem is this. If we compare the texts of the first three Gospels in a Synopsis (a book which sets out the first three Gospels in parallel columns) we discover remarkable similarities and agreements among them, such that their accounts are often almost word for word identical. We also discover striking disagreements between them: different versions of Jesus' sayings, different versions of events, and indeed a considerable amount of material which is not shared by all three, or indeed which occurs in only one Gospel. How do we account for these agreements and disagreements?

Writing just over 120 years ago, Bishop Christopher Wordsworth felt he could explain the agreements by appealing to the divine authorship of the Spirit who used the principle of repetition to inculcate divine truth (as indeed he did in the Old Testament where prophecies and psalms are found in different though largely identical versions). The differences, on the other hand, could be explained partly by the fact that Jesus spoke in 'Syro-Chaldaic' (Aramaic) whereas the Evangelists wrote in Greek; partly by the inadequacy of human words to express the full meaning of the divine wisdom, so that the Holy Spirit offered different versions to uncover the fuller meaning of the sayings.

To be reminded of such arguments is to realize how far opinions have changed in academic circles in a hundred years. His account is remarkable enough in that it solidly refuses to countenance the source-critical studies which had been pursued with such vigour in Germany throughout the nineteenth century. My own copy adds a twist to this. It was given by C.H. Dodgson (Lewis Carroll) to his nephew. It is revealing that such a formidable logician and story-teller should have been satisfied with such explanations.

Wordsworth's account is problematic for at least two main reasons. First, it allows human agency in the writing of the Gospel a very uncertain and partial role. As far as the agreements between them are concerned, the Evangelists are mere mouthpieces of the Spirit. The disagreements, however,

are partly accounted for by the human process of translation
from one language to another, partly by the Spirit's agency in
providing the kind of variety which will reveal the true
meaning of Jesus' words. Secondly, it ignores what are much
more evident explanations of such agreements and disagreements, evident, that is, if we regard the Evangelists as
authors in their own right: the use of literary sources, of
different oral traditions in which the stories and sayings had
been modified in the course of transmission. The interesting
thing is that it was only after these other kinds of explanation had been thoroughly investigated and accepted by most
scholars that it was possible to go on and see the Evangelists
as just that: authors in their own right.

What sorts of explanations can we then offer of such agreements and disagreements? Consider for a moment a striking
example of verbal agreements which made headlines after
the Poll tax riots. In the trial of Roy Hanney (a TV production engineer with no previous convictions) the two police
witnesses agreed uncannily in the statements which they
made, supposedly independently, on the evening of the riot.
Here is how The Observer of November 11th 1990 presented
them:

'The Damning Statements'

The following are the beginnings of the accounts supposedly
written independently on 31 March

PC EGAN: 'We were deployed on a short shield cordon attempting to push a violent crowd of 500 plus north in Charing Cross Road, WC 1. All the time we were under prolonged attack of missiles consisting of bricks, bottles, pieces of concrete and coins. The order was given to charge into the extremely violent crowd. As we moved forward I saw a man whom I now know to be Roy Hanney. He was wearing an army-type jacket which was

PC RAMSAY: 'We were deployed as a short shield unit forming a cordon attempting to push a violent crowd of about 500 plus north in Charing Cross Road. We were under constant fire from numerous missiles including brick, bottles, sticks and metal bars. The order was given to charge into a violent crowd, as we moved forward, I noticed a man I now know to be Roy Hanney. He had a close-cropped head an and army combat jacket on. He came to zipped up, and he had closely shaven fair hair. As he came to the front of the crowd I saw him shouting something at us which I could not hear, due to the noise of the crowd. I then saw Hanney pull his right arm back and throw what appeared to be a lump of concrete into the police cordon.'

the forefront of the crowd shouting and swearing at us. I could not make out what he was saying but he shouted it in an aggressive manner. I then noticed him draw back his right arm and throw what appeared to be a brick into the police cordon. Myself and PC Egan ran forward with other officers towards Hanney.'

Not unreasonably, at the trial, the Defence Counsel questioned the independence of the two accounts. 'PC Ramsay denied emphatically having copied PC Egan's statement. *But the structure of the two statements, and much of their phraseology, was identical, down to a mistake about the day of the incident—both said Sunday, not Saturday.*' In response PC Ramsay said that the similarities were 'coincidence' and pointed to the different descriptions of Hanney's hairstyle: 'close-cropped', as opposed to 'shaven'. 'Mr. Dias asked him to look at his handwritten original. PC Ramsay had crossed out "shaven" and substituted "close-cropped". Most of the jurors reacted with laughter.' Shortly afterwards, in a rare legal move, the jury intervened to stop the trial.

The point here, of course, is not to compare the motives of the Evangelists with those of PCs Egan and Ramsay but rather to compare the modes of production of the two statements and the Synoptic Gospels. It is hard to see how this mixture of agreement and disagreement could have come about other than by someone copying and making minor changes to a written document. They might of course both have been copying from the same document; the point is that they were, or at least one of them was, copying from a *written document. There is, that is to say, a relationship of literary dependence between the two*, without which it would be hard to explain the agreements in structure, syntax, phraseology, detail and mistakes between the two accounts.

Certainly one explanation which the jury ruled out in the Poll tax trial was that the two accounts were the independent work of two eye-witnesses. Nor, quite reasonably, did they consider whether the policemen were simply recounting a popular and well-known story about the riot. That was not being claimed and there clearly had not been time for such stories to become widespread. However, for the Synoptic Gospels, written some 30 or more years after the event, this might be a possible explanation. Perhaps the sources of the Synoptic Gospels were in a measure oral sources, oral traditions which had been circulating in a relatively stable form for some time and which were recorded in their own way (with, that is, minor variations) by the Evangelists. This is a by no means impossible but, in view of the close verbal agreements, still less likely explanation than that what we have in the Synoptic Gospels is the result of some kind of literary dependence.

Of course, it is one thing to come to the conclusion that there is a literary relationship between the Synoptic Gospels, quite another to decide how the relationships ran. Who, in simple terms was copying whom? Were there other documents involved? What role if any did well-established oral tradition have in shaping the Gospels? We shall not spend long over this question. There is a strong consensus among the majority of scholars as well as a persistent, if small, band of doubters. We shall then simply set out the majority view and look at a few objections.

Since the end of the last century in Germany and at the latest since B.H. Streeter's *Four Gospels* (1924) in this country, the accepted view has been that Mark wrote his Gospel first, drawing on material which came to him largely by word of mouth (whether from Peter or some more widespread fund of stories about and sayings of Jesus is still debated) and a Passion narrative which had already received fairly fixed form in the liturgy of the church; that Matthew and Luke used Mark as the basis and framework of their Gospels but also used a written collection of sayings—generally called Q—together with some material of their own. This is known as the two document hypothesis and can be represented diagrammatically as follows:

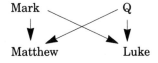

One of the simplest ways to see the force of this explanation is to look at Alan Barr's *Diagram of Synoptic Relationships*. What this shows can be summarized as follows:

1. Virtually all of Mark appears in either Matthew or Luke. Matthew omits:

Mk 1.23-28	Synagogue at Capernaum
1.35-38	Withdrawal of Jesus
9.38-40	Strange Exorcist
12.41-44	Widow's mite

Luke omits:

Mk 6.17-29	Death of the Baptist
6.45–8.21	From the Walking on the Sea to the Leaven of the Pharisees
8.32-33	Rebuke to Peter
9.9b-13	Conversation on Elijah
9.28-29	Power of prayer
10.1-12	Marriage and divorce
10.35-40	Sons of Zebedee
11.12-14, 20-25	Cursing and withering of the fig-tree.

Both omit:

Mk 3.20-21	Crowd presses
4.26-29	Seed growing secretly (?//Mt 13.24-30)
5.4-5	Demoniac's fetters
8.22-26	Blind man of Bethsaida
9.15-16	Exchange between Jesus and crowd
9.21-24	Exchange between Jesus and father
9.49-50	Salt (Mt 5.13; Lk 14.34-35)
14.51-52	Young man at arrest.

2. The order of the Markan material in Luke is very close to that in Mark itself. Only the following passages occur in different order:

Lk. 6.12-16	Mk 3.13-19	Appointment of the Twelve
8.19-21	3.31-35	Jesus' Mother and Brethren
22.56-62	14.66-72	Peter's Denials

3. Matthew follows Mark's order closely though there are a substantial number of displacements in the first half of the Gospel:

Mt.	4.23	Mk	1.39; 3.7-8	Preaching and healing
	7.28-29		1.22	Effect of preaching
	8.14-17		1.29-34	Healing of Peter's mother-in-law; healings in evening
	8.23-24		4.35–5.17(20)	Stilling of Storm; Gadarene Demoniac
	9.18-26		5.21-43	Jairus's daughter; woman with issue of blood
	10.1-4		6.7; 3.13-19	Appointment of Twelve
	10.9-14		6.8-11	Mission of Twelve
	21.18-19		11.12-14	Cursing and withering of fig tree

4. Where Matthew and Luke have material in common there is less overall agreement in order than in any of the above cases, but still significant agreement in order.

None of this of course adds up to a simple proof of the two document hypothesis. Arguments based on order are easy to turn round. If Matthew had been written first, there would of course still be very considerable agreement in order between the three. But then we would have to look at alternative views of the relations between the three. Suppose, as some would suggest (e.g. W.R. Farmer, reviving the Griesbach hypothesis), that the relationships went:

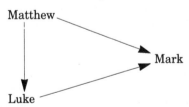

Then we would have a situation where (a) Luke had made much more radical changes to the order of Matthew than on the former hypothesis he had made to Mark (for now we would suppose that he was taking his 'Q' material from Matthew; (b) Mark had largely followed Luke's order but had on occasion (in the Passion narrative) preferred Matthew's; and c)—most difficult of all—Mark had chosen to omit large parts of Matthew and Luke, the infancy stories, great blocks of teaching material and the resurrection accounts.

Augustine and others have suggested that Mark was an

abbreviator, something like a digest writer, which, it is asserted, was not uncommon in the ancient world. But then we have to look at the accounts in rather more detail. The fact is that where all three have the same accounts, Mark's is often longer, containing extra details which an abbreviator would hardly have added. This then presents Mark as a poor literary craftsman, whereas his work is a remarkable piece of natural storytelling.

This is to say that the cumulative effect of the observations above (and of course of a great deal of more detailed observations) is to favour the two document hypothesis based on Markan priority. It might then seem that we can be confident that where Matthew differs from Mark we have evidence of Matthew's modification of Mark. As Graham Stanton has recently argued (*A Gospel for a New People*, pp. 36-41), there are difficulties with this which may make us somewhat cautious about our use of the two document hypothesis in exegesis of the Gospels.

1.   The minor agreements. There are a number of cases in the so-called triple tradition, that is, where all three have the same material, where Matthew and Luke agree against Mark, either in offering a slightly differing account or in both omitting part of Mark's account altogether. The differences are not great, more the kind of fine editorial adjustments which an editor would make to the text. Why then did Matthew and Luke both, independently of each other as our hypothesis demands, make the same kind of minor adjustments? This kind of challenge can only be met by detailed argument. In many cases the minor agreements can be shown to be fairly obvious kinds of changes to make. But a look at the omissions which both Luke and Matthew have in common, listed above under (1) may perhaps be better explained by the existence of slightly differing versions of Mark at the time of the writing of Matthew and Luke. This view is supported by the existence of similar different versions of contemporary documents, such as *The Testament of the Twelve Patriarchs, Life of Adam, Testament of Job*.

2. We cannot be confident in every case that we can establish the final form of the text of Matthew. Stanton lists 9.34; 13.14-15; 16.2b-3; 21.44 as doubtfully original and 21.29-31 as 'in disarray' (p. 37). It may well be that the present form of the Matthaean text has been influenced by the Lucan parallel.

3. It is also not possible to be sure to what extent Matthew's other sources, Q and his special material and even Mark, had already undergone change and redaction before he came to them.

4. It may also be that Matthew's Gospel as we know it now contains redaction which occurred after the Evangelist had completed his work on it.

5. Some of the differences between Matthew and Mark and Q may be explained by the continuing existence of the oral tradition which lay behind those sources. If Matthew had just heard a story in a variant version, he may have preferred, unconsciously or consciously, some detail which was not in his written source.

What this means cumulatively is not insignificant, perhaps even more significant that Stanton would allow. At the very least it means that in any case where there are minor variations between Matthew and his sources we cannot simply take this as a benchmark of Matthew's own theology. It may be no more than the reflection of a difference in his version of Mark or in the continuing oral tradition. Only if we can build up a consistent pattern in such variations can we be sure that we have evidence for Matthew's own viewpoint. So much Stanton would largely concede. But does it not mean more than this? Does it not mean that there are far fewer cases where we can be sure that we have redactional modifications by the Evangelist? The details of Matthaean redaction may now be less the benchmark of his theology than part of the evidence which has to be carefully weighed alongside the evidence of his arrangement of his sources, of his composition as a whole. I shall return to these thoughts when discussing literary approaches to the Gospel later in the chapter.

There is one other area which exercises some scholars and that is the question of Q. Was it a written document or a relatively discrete oral tradition? Is such an hypothesis necessary at all? Arguments for a written document have to be based principally on evidence of common order between Matthew and Luke. Here the problem is that there is not the same degree of order in the Q material as there is in the Markan material. What there is, however, is by no means unimpressive. This suggests to many that there were different versions of Q circulating and that Matthew and Luke used different versions. This is further supported by the very considerable differences in wording and phraseology between some of the material in Matthew and Luke. The more one becomes aware of these differences, however, the more one might feel inclined to see Q as a relatively coherent body of oral tradition, rather than as a series of documents. This simply reinforces the points made above about the need for caution in judgments about Matthew's editorial work. The less certain we are about the form of Q which Matthew used, the less confident we can be about Matthew's redaction of it, which of course does not stop some scholars from putting forward very detailed reconstructions of different editions of Q.

More radically some scholars would want to dispense with Q altogether (Farrer, Goulder, Drury). The real problems with such proposals, which are in many ways most attractive, lie in the way Luke is then thought to have edited Matthew. As this is not strictly a problem for this guide, we shall merely note the point and pass on.

Literary Characteristics

We have just seen that doubt about our ability to know the precise form of the sources which Matthew was working on means that we have to be cautious when making judgments about his detailed redaction. Such judgments need to be set alongside the views we may form about his composition of the Gospel as a whole. Matthew, after all, did not simply work on the small scale, making little changes to his received sources here and there (though he certainly did that); he also put together large blocks of material, drawing on a variety of sources to compose a work we call a Gospel, and which is one of a number of such works.

The questions which flow quite naturally from this are: first, what was it to compose a Gospel? What sort of book did Matthew have it in mind to write? And secondly, how did he set about arranging the sources at his disposal into a book? What principles (if that is the right word) of composition did he employ?

It is important to know what sort of a book one is reading if one wants to grasp its meaning fully. The form is an integral part of the way in which a writer communicates to his readers. It may be more or less simple; more or less fixed and rigid. A sonnet is a complex form with very strict rules; a novel or short story much less fixed and capable of both considerable simplicity and considerable complexity. But in all cases it matters whether or not we realize what the form is. If we think we are reading a traveller's tale and it is really a novel, we may well miss some of the pointers which the writer has given us which are important to the development of the narrative. Our expectations will be different and therefore we may not give attention to aspects of what is being said.

Writers too need to be aware of the rules which govern the literary forms which they employ. They need to know what their readers' expectations might be in order to get their attention, to communicate easily, but also to surprise and puzzle. Creative writers may well remodel the literary forms or genres with which they work; but they still need to work broadly within the literary conventions of their day.

Therefore, when we come to consider an ancient literary work like the Gospel of Matthew we want to know as much as we can about its form, that is to say about the then existing literary conventions which governed this kind of writing.

This question is not nearly so abstract as it might seem. Literary conventions do not (often) exist in some kind of rule book, though critics may try to tabulate and analyse them. They exist in living communities of writers and readers; they require, that is to say, a 'literary public'. On occasion, as with some Greek and Roman literature of the time, such a public would be sophisticated and educated, a wealthy elite meeting in each other's houses for public readings of the latest literary works: poetry, memoirs, lives, letters, dialogues. In other cases the public will have been more extensive, as with the audiences of plays and comedies in the ancient world. Not all will perhaps have appreciated the finer points of form, but most will have had at least an intuitive grasp of the genre and known broadly what to expect in the development of, respectively, a tragedy and a comedy. Other works will have been more at home in religious communities of different kinds: liturgies, psalms, narratives, legal material, and these will have had their proper context and rules which will have had to be observed.

So we need to ask: What sort of 'literary public' was Matthew's Gospel written for? *and* What other models of literary production did Matthew have before him when he wrote? The questions are interrelated and the first will occupy us considerably in the next chapter, but still here we need to give some provisional answers. Let us take the question of literary models first.

Obviously, when Matthew wrote, his principal (one of his principal?) model(s) was Mark but what kind of a book was that? Mark's book starts: 'The beginning of the gospel of Jesus Christ...' Scholars are generally agreed that 'gospel' here refers to the Christian message which Mark's book will relate, not to the type of book—a Gospel—which Mark was beginning to write. They are rather less in agreement about what kind of book it was that Mark wrote.

One obvious parallel to Mark's Gospel might be thought to lie in ancient biography. This view was widely held in the nineteenth century but was questioned earlier this century, notably by German form-critics who argued (1) that the Gospels were folk literature rather than high literature; (2) that the 'literary understanding of the Synoptics begins with the recognition that they are collections of material. The composers are only to the smallest extent authors. They are principally collectors, vehicles of tradition, editors' (M. Dibelius, *From Tradition to Gospel*, p. 3). That is, the Gospels, were in form (if not in content) more like collections of Faust legends, for example, than like literary biographies.

However, as interest in the editorial activity of the Evangelists has grown since the end of the war, so this sharp distinction between the literary forms of the Hellenistic world and the Gospels has come to be challenged. Some, notably David Aune (*The New Testament in its Literary Environment*), have argued that the Gospels should be seen as examples of Graeco-Roman biography at a popular level. Aune states that such biography tends to be in the form of 'complex or host genres serving as literary frames for a variety of shorter forms' (p. 28) and stresses the great variety of such biographical forms, while indicating many striking analogies in the content, motifs and purposes of ancient biographical literature and the Gospels. Others, like Ernest Best (*Mark: The Gospel as Story*, pp. 140ff.), have suggested that the closest literary parallels to Mark are to be found in Old Testament narrative cycles, like the Elisha–Elijah cycle. This view can find considerable support, not least in the analogies between the particular stories and motifs associated with the central figures: cures of lepers, feeding of crowds, raising of the dead.

This is a difficult debate to summarize or indeed to adjudicate. What the form critics saw rightly (as is stressed again by Best) is that the Evangelists, notably Mark, were 'preservers of the tradition' (*Mark: The Gospel as Story*, pp. 109-22), that they collected it and treated it with respect and made only relatively modest alterations to it. They saw too, and this is agreed by Aune, that the works they produced were written in popular style and, certainly in Mark's case, could lay no claim to being works of sophisticated literature. Thus they compared them (so especially K.L. Schmidt, 'Stellung') to later collections of legends and sayings, The Sayings of the Fathers, the Legends of St Francis and the collections of Faust Legends, rather than to the more carefully organized (whether chronologically or topically) lives of ancient biography. But the form-critics' interest in the traditions which the Evangelists collected led them to ignore the sense in which they had composed a work which was more than the sum of its parts. Mark's narrative is a powerful and moving piece of writing and this is missed if one simply analyses out the 'framework' which he constructed to contain his collection of stories and sayings and presents it as a rather crude literary expedient.

Thus Aune is right to explore the contemporary literary parallels to the Gospels. Few writers produce powerful works of literature, whether polished or not, without some literary models. Contemporary *Lives* are one obvious source of such models for the Evangelists, particularly if we allow that writers may draw on such models freely and creatively. Of course the freer we allow them to have been, the more difficult it is to decide which model they were following. One does not have to come down on one side or another. Mark may well have been influenced by contemporary *Lives* and have formed the wish to write such a *Life* to justify and commend the way of the Gospel to its followers. But it would be strange if someone so obviously steeped in the Scriptures had not learnt something of his narrative craft from the great stories of the Pentateuch and the books of Samuel and Kings.

But if Mark is Matthew's closest model when he starts to write, what other influences shaped his work? Stanton (*Gospel for a New People*, pp. 66-71) has argued interestingly that Matthew takes up and develops the genre of both Mark and Q. Q (here Stanton follows Kloppenborg, *The Formation of Q*) is a collection of wisdom sayings which is a genre widely found in ancient Near Eastern writing. It is also like the collections of chreiae (anecdotes) in Greek. Both these forms may have 'a biographical interest' and so it is possible that Q itself had with the addition of the temptation narrative developed closer to ancient *Lives*. Thus when Matthew takes it up, so Stanton, he does not simply destroy it by incorporating it into Mark. In the first place it is not, as we have just noted, a completely alien form. Secondly, although Matthew reorganizes his Q material more freely than (it is generally accepted) does Luke, he does so in a way which preserves (at least in part) the genre of Q. By creating a series of distinct discourses which are signalled as such at the end of each section by very similar phrases: 'when Jesus had finished these sayings' (7.28; 11.1; 13.53; 19.1; 26.1), Matthew creates smaller versions of Q within his narrative framework. At the same time he extends the Markan genre by incorporating more discourse material which is arranged topically.

One way of bringing these kinds of discussion into focus is to ask, what was the literary structure of the Gospel? The question here is often put but the word structure is one which tends to be overworked. What exactly is meant?

'Structure' is a word which suggests some kind of geometrical or otherwise regular configuration of materials. It is applied readily to building design and other forms of construction, but can be easily used figuratively of arguments, works of music and literature. In all cases one is looking for some kind of patterning which is linked to some purpose or intention: the construction of a strong, elegant, durable building, or the creation of a work of art of beauty and clarity. It is in this fairly broad and obvious figurative sense that it is most obviously used by New Testament scholars. This is quite different from its use among a particular school of 'structuralist' literary critics, who were looking for ways in which texts, rituals and other products of the human mind were thought to betray certain 'deep structures' which are determined by the mind's own inherent patterns of thought. We shall then ask: what evidence is there of some shaping by Matthew of his material and in what sense does this betray any kind of rational purpose?

We have already noticed certain characteristics of Matthew's use of his sources, Mark and Q. We saw that in his use of Mark he sometimes departs from Mark's order in the first part of his Gospel, while following the order very closely from ch. 11 onwards. We also saw that Matthew had constructed a number of discourses: chs. 5–7 the Sermon on the Mount; ch. 10 the mission discourse; ch. 13 parables; ch. 18 advice for the community; ch. (23)24–25 judgment and the End. Much of the material in these sections comes from his other sources, Q and his own special material. Thus we can say very simply that Matthew has followed Mark closely, though he has rearranged some of the material in the earlier chapters, notably to give an extended section on miracles in ch. 8–9; and that he has fitted a series of extended discourses into this largely given narrative framework.

One of the earliest explanations of this pattern was offered by an American scholar, B.S. Bacon (*Studies in Matthew*). He suggested that Matthew had deliberately constructed five books each with a narrative section and a discourse of Jesus by way of comparison with the Pentateuch, so as to suggest that Jesus was the new Moses. That such patterning is deliberate is shown easily by Matthew's use of a recurring phrase: 'when Jesus had finished these sayings' (7.28; 11.1; 13.53; 19.1), culminating in 'when Jesus had finished all these sayings' in 26.1, to mark off the end of each section. Such patterning cannot be accidental. What more obvious purpose should Matthew have here than to compare Jesus' teaching with the Law given by Moses? The contrast is again brought out clearly in the Sermon on the Mount in the antitheses between 'you have heard it said of old' and 'but I say unto you'. In all this, as Graham Stanton has suggested recently, Matthew is using a familiar and favorite rhetorical device of the day, comparison (*sugkrisis, Gospel for a New People*, pp. 77-84; see too D.C. Allison, *The New Moses*).

There are, however, difficulties with Bacon's account. First, there is no place in his scheme for the infancy narratives of chs. 1–2 and the passion and resurrection narratives of ch. 26–28. While it may be not unreasonable to treat the infancy narratives as a kind of prologue, it will hardly do to treat the expanded Markan passion and resurrection account as an epilogue. Secondly, the scheme seems to leave out some of the discourse material, 11.7-30 and 23.1-39, though the latter may, of course, be regarded as part of the fifth discourse. Further, it has been questioned whether the recurring phrase 'when Jesus had finished...' is a *concluding* phrase rather than a transitional one; and lastly it is disputed whether the Gospel gives any evidence for Matthew's thinking of Jesus as a 'new Moses'.

Perhaps the real problem with Bacon's analysis is that it tries to solve too much. It proposes a schema for the whole book, rather than offering an explanation for Matthew's arrangement of his discourse material within the Markan framework. If it is revised, to assert that Matthew's intention in placing these five major blocks of teaching evenly through the Gospel is to stress the importance of Jesus' teaching— and indeed to compare it with the Mosaic Law, then most of the objections will fall. Even the objection that the phrase itself is not strictly a concluding phrase, even to a discourse on its own, is hardly telling. In the first place it clearly does refer to the fact that Jesus had concluded his teaching; secondly, even if it is true that it inaugurates the next section, it is still a clear marker, delineating the start of a new section, and hence the end of another.

Such a revision of Bacon's thesis leaves unexplained the nature of Matthew's narrative scheme and purpose. We have seen that he largely takes over Mark's framework, but also that he makes certain changes in the first half of the Gospel. J.D. Kingsbury (*Matthew: Structure, Christology, Kingdom*) has suggested that we may find a clue to Matthew's narrative purpose in another recurring phrase: 'From then on Jesus began...' True, this phrase only recurs once after its first use in 4.17, namely at 16.21. Nevertheless, the two occurrences mark off, in the first instance, Jesus' ministry from the ministry of John the Baptist; and in the second, the move from Jesus' ministry to his death and resurrection. That is to say, this schema draws the readers' attention to the different stages in salvation history which occur in the Gospel. It demonstrates to Kingsbury that Matthew is primarily concerned with his narrative rather than with the teaching material.

There are considerable problems with this view. 4.17 is not an entirely obvious division between John the Baptist and Jesus. This seems more readily to occur at 4.12. Nor indeed is 16.21 the most obvious point at which to mark the transition to the Passion. 26.1, one of the occurrences of the other phrase, would be just as suitable.

Lastly, and most seriously, it seems strange to suggest that Matthew is *exalting* narrative over discourse, when he has taken such care in the construction of his major discourse sections and their insertion into his Markan source. Clearly Matthew is unlike his source 'Q' in that he produces a work in which there is a balance of narrative and discourse material but it would be a serious mistake to underestimate the importance of his discourse material, as a comparison with Mark makes clear. In his earlier work, Kingsbury rejected such a comparison. We should allow Matthew to stand for itself. This is puzzling. Why should we ignore some of the most striking evidence that we have, namely that there is a relationship of literary dependence between Mark and Matthew and that in all likelihood it is Matthew that has used Mark? This must affect our view of his literary purposes, particularly where we are concerned with structure. If he has rearranged or modified existing structures, that must tell us something about his intentions.

What we do know is that he has modified his Markan framework somewhat differently at different stages of the Gospel, more at first, only by way of insertion in the latter half. The earlier modifications principally serve the purpose of gathering together much of the miracle material into a section (chs. 8–9). Some have seen in this a presentation of Jesus as the Messiah of deed to complement the presentation of him as Messiah of Word in chs. 5–7. This would fit quite neatly with the suggestion that in modifying Mark's Gospel Matthew has followed patterns of contemporary *Lives* which arranged matters topically. It would of course also say something about Matthew's christology.

Further, the contrast between his use of Mark in the two halves of the Gospel would suggest that Matthew is less than wholly consistent in his restructuring of Mark and that we should be content to discover what design we can without seeking a total explanation for every aspect of the Gospel. This view is advocated persuasively by Stanton. In particular, Stanton (*Gospel for a New People*, pp. 71-76) has suggested that such an approach to the Gospel does justice to its original mode of delivery. Such texts, so Stanton, would have been primarily read aloud in public. The length of the Gospel would have made it unlikely that it was often read on one occasion in its entirety. So that while people may have picked up detailed points of arrangement within sections, they would have been less able to see overall structures, and Matthew equally would have been less concerned with intricate overall structures.

Against this others have still thought to see very intricate structural patterns in the Gospel. Davies and Allison in their recent commentary have suggested that chiasm (arrangements of material which are patterned in the form a b c b1 a1 and variants thereof) plays a significant role in its structure and have arranged the whole Gospel chiastically with its centre at ch. 13. This requires too much detailed discussion here. There is always a certain subjectivity in spotting chiasm, though it is not to be ignored. Matthew may well have used it as a device on the small scale, but its use to structure the whole Gospel given its manner of composition by 'pasting together' various sources is unlikely.

Finally, in this section we need to say something briefly about Matthew's audience. Who, in his own view, was he writing for?

We noted in passing that Mark's Gospel was stylistically rough. This is hardly an indication that it was written for a cultivated literary public. Its readers were probably members of house-churches in Graeco-Roman cities who were for the most part less than well educated, though there may have been some for whom Mark's Gospel came across as unpolished. Was Matthew attempting to bring Mark's Gospel more into line with the cultural milieu of the Hellenistic city? Quite possibly. Luke, writing his preface to Theophilus, certainly gave himself the airs of a Hellenistic historian (Lk. 1.1-4). But was Matthew writing primarily for an educated Greek audience?

This is a question we shall explore further in the next chapter but there are some points to be made here. The fact that Matthew is concerned to improve Mark's style, that he writes with conscious literary purpose, is significant. It shows him as wishing to conform to certain literary standards and it is reasonable to infer from this that there were those among his audience who would have been able to appreciate the value of what he was doing. Who were they? Were they Jews or Gentiles? The simple answer is that they might have been either. There are some notable examples of educated Jews writing in Greek: Philo and Josephus. Thus we can make no easy move from that fact that Matthew wrote educated Greek to the religious background of his readers. More significant may well be his use of the Old Testament. Appeal to the fulfilment of Old Testament prophecy as vindication of one's story does not necessarily mean that one assumes that one's readers accept the authority of the Scriptures. Fulfilment of prophecy—any prophecy—might in itself be enough to convince many. Nevertheless Matthew's appeal to the Old Testament on such a regular basis does suggest, at the least, that it was his natural point of reference and authority and might well also suggest that his community was well able to identify with the religious authority of the Scriptures quoted. Can we go further and suggest that his community was some kind of scholarly community eager to seek out the meaning of the Scriptures, a school of Matthew? We will take up these questions again in the next chapter.

Reading the Gospel of Matthew

The kind of work we have been considering so far has been principally concerned with the sources, composition and literary genre of the Gospels. Recent studies of Matthew have included a good number of literary-critical studies which have claimed to be essentially distinct from such studies. The term 'literary-critical' is itself a little confusing in the context of biblical studies, for it was originally used to refer to such matters as we have discussed above under the heading of source-criticism. It was, that is to say, concerned with the biblical texts from an historical point of view, exploring their genesis, the manner in which they came to be written. More recently, however, such historical concerns have been contrasted with a literary mode of studying texts, which in its extreme form is wholly uninterested in the historical genesis or reception of texts.

This is, I think, unhelpful. Literary studies of Matthew may be written from many different theoretical perspectives: some scholars may attempt a reading of the Gospel which uses the canons of modern narrative theory; others may be much more interested in attempting to trace out the literary conventions of the time and to follow the history of the text's' reception. They may both shed light on the text.

Certainly, it seems to me indisputable that biblical scholarship needs to take the Gospels seriously as works of literature. Simply to see them as repositories of Christian doctrine; or worse to see them solely as evidence for the life of the early Christian communities would be to ignore their

character as stories, just as it would be to ignore the very
different quality of their telling. In this respect studies like
those of J.D. Kingsbury (*Matthew as Story*), R.A. Edwards
(*Matthew's Story of Jesus*) and D.B. Howell (*Matthew's
Inclusive Story*) have been valuable in reminding us of the
narrative character of the Gospel.

The question which such studies raise is: what kinds of
narratives are gospels? Do we see them as somehow timeless
works which can yield up their secrets to modern
understandings of narrative? Do we see them as works which
are indebted to the literary canons of their own time and
which therefore can fully be understood only when we appreciate the rhetoric and indeed the manner of their production?

It may not be inappropriate at this point to invoke a
Matthaean maxim: 'By their fruits you shall know them.'
Reading gospels from the point of view of modern narrative
theory alerts us to features of the text we might well otherwise miss. Thus in Howell's book we are invited to consider
the way in which the Evangelist organizes his material
according to a certain 'point of view'; to explore the way in
which certain key themes such as promise/fulfillment or
acceptance/rejection are emplotted in the narrative; above all
to consider the way in which the reader is drawn into the
story, not so much by identifying with any particular character in the narrative, as for example the disciples, but by
coming to see Jesus himself as the model for discipleship. We
are encouraged, that is to say, not simply to see the Gospel as
propounding a particular view of history, a particular christology, but as a complex rhetorical strategy for winning over
its readers.

There is a great deal of detailed discussion in Howell's
book and it is possible here only to look at one instance of the
application of these notions to the Gospel. Howell sees the
opening section of the Gospel as serving to produce certain
competencies in the reader by introducing the major characters, adumbrating the conflict between Jesus and his opponents and establishing the plotting devices which are used
throughout the narrative (p. 115). Thus the genealogy is
used to place Jesus firmly in the history of Abraham and
David and in ch. 2 the theme of Abraham is taken up again

as Jesus is shown as 'heir to the promise of blessing to the Gentiles'. Above all the genealogy and its summary points to the providential purposes of God which are being fulfilled in Jesus and so introduces us to one of the two main plotting devices, which along with the notion of acceptance/fulfilment, controls the development of the narrative.

We need not follow all the detail of Howell's exposition of Mt. 1.1–4.16 but an example or two of how he sees these motifs operating may be useful. In the stories relating the birth and naming of Jesus, 'Joseph is confronted with the choice of either accepting or rejecting the angel's instructions' (p. 117). Because of Joseph's obedience the 'will of God is fulfilled in the predictive sense in that his pre-determined plan is carried out—but is also fulfilled in the volitional sense, in that divine instructions are accepted and executed by Joseph' (p. 117). There is, that is to say, a neat intertwining of the two motifs which can also be observed elsewhere.

As the story develops, so the contrast between those who accept like Joseph and the Magi and those who reject like Herod is played out and interwoven with the motif of fulfilment which is provided largely, but not entirely, by the fulfilment citations which occur freely in this section. So too with John the Baptist, whose conflict with the Pharisees and Sadducees is initiated by his denunciation of them in 3.8, which Howell says 'contains the suggestion about what called forth the condemnation: their actions were incongruous with true repentance' (p. 122). By contrast Matthew does not use the theme of rejection but rather 'uses the theme of acceptance to plot Jesus' baptism. Jesus' response to John in 3.15a, which for the evangelist provides the answer to the question of how Jesus could submit to John for baptism, highlights the theme of acceptance' (p. 123).

And so Howell's treatment of the 'narrative temporal ordering and emplotment' proceeds. The last remark may help to focus some of the reservations which I feel about this kind of discussion. To say that the discussion between Jesus and John at the baptism 'highlights the theme of acceptance' is clearly not false—but is it sufficient? The exchange clearly highlights a good deal more: on the one hand it contrasts

Jesus and John, on the other it unites them in their mutual acceptance of God's will whereby they 'fulfil all righteousness'. As Luz points out, the reference to all righteousness transcends the situation of the baptism: it now refers to the total will of God which *all* are commanded to do (*Matthew 1–7*, p. 178). By accepting, Jesus becomes the example to Christians. At the same time John's acquiescence also points to the way in which Jesus is to be emulated. Now clearly this is entirely consistent with what Howell says. He explicitly supports an exemplary reading of the passage against a salvation historical one: Jesus' baptism marks a key point in the divine plan. My concern is that Howell's rather timeless mode of proceeding, by invoking generalized notions of emplotment, overlooks contemporary literary conventions which might have drawn out other important aspects of the texts. Graham Stanton has drawn attention (*Gospel for a New People*, pp. 77-84) to Matthew's use of comparison which was a widely used rhetorical device. By the same token, there is no doubt that his exemplary reading gains much support from contemporary linguistic evidence which shows that 'righteousness' undergoes a change in meaning from its biblical sense of 'God's saving and righteous order' to 'righteousness' understood as an ethical norm to be fulfilled by men and women.

What this raises then is a wider set of questions as to whether there is not more to be learnt from at least a combination of modes of interpretation based on modern literary theory with those which pay greater attention to the literary conventions which were in force at the time when the Gospels were written. More, we should also consider what we know about the mode of production of the Gospel: the way in which Matthew worked with his sources, the extent to which he was free and/or constrained by the community for which he wrote. And finally, none of this should distract us from the solid philological task of determining the lingusitic conventions which were in force when Matthew wrote.

Conclusion

The conclusions of this chapter may be briefly drawn together. Matthew's Gospel is a complex variant of Mark's.

He has taken an existing work and reworked it. Stylistically he has improved Mark's rather rough Greek. Structurally he has woven into it a substantial amount of discourse material, creating five blocks of teaching material reminiscent of the five books of the Law. He has also reordered some of Mark's original Gospel to give a certain grouping of Jesus' deeds in chs. 8–9. In this Matthew has not substantially altered the form of Mark's work: it remains a book that, like the ancient Hellenistic biographies, is a 'host genre': a broad narrative capable of accommodating many different forms. Like Mark it draws on the Old Testament. But there is a slackening of Mark's narrative tension and pace which shows Matthew as perhaps more interested in the discourse material drawn from his other main source 'Q'. In this, he is of course also less close to the Old Testament and closer to the Jewish writers who would compile the Mishnah at the end of the century. Thus already this consideration of the literary character of the Gospel suggests its proximity to contemporary Jewish concerns about the interpretation and teaching of the Law.

Further Reading

D.C. Allison, *The New Moses: A Matthean Typology* (Minneapolis: Augsburg Fortress, 1993).

D. Aune, *The New Testament in its Literary Environment* (Philadelphia: Westminster Press, 1987).

B.S. Bacon, *Studies in Matthew* (London: Constable, 1930).

A. Barr, *Diagram of Synoptic Relationships* (Edinburgh: T. & T. Clark, 1938).

E. Best, *Mark: The Gospel as Story* (Edinburgh: T. & T. Clark, 1983).

M. Dibelius, *From Tradition to Gospel* (London: Ivor Nicholson and Watson, 1934).

J.H. Drury, *Tradition and Design in Luke's Gospel* (London: Darton, Longman and Todd, 1976).

R.A. Edwards, *Matthew's Story of Jesus* (Philadelphia: Fortress Press, 1985).

W.R. Farmer, *The Synoptic Problem* (New York: Macmillan, 1976).

A.M. Farrer, 'On Dispensing with Q', in D. Nineham (ed.), *Studies in the Gospels* (Oxford: Basil Blackwell, 1955), pp. 55-86.

M.D. Goulder, *Midrash and Lection in Matthew* (London: SPCK, 1974).

D.B. Howell, *Matthew's Inclusive Story* (Sheffield: JSOT Press, 1990).

J.D. Kingsbury, *Matthew: Structure, Christology, Kingdom* (Philadelphia: Fortress Press, 1975).

—*Matthew as Story* (Philadelphia: Fortress Press, 1986).

J. Kloppenborg, *The Formation of Q* (Philadelphia: Fortress Press, 1987).

K.L. Schmidt, 'Die Stellung der Evangelien in der allgemeinen Literaturgeschichte', in H. Schmidt (ed.), *EUCHARISTERION: Studien zur Religion und Literatur des Alten und Neuen Testaments, Hermann Gunkel zum 60. Geburtstag* (FRLANT, 36; Göttingen: Vandenhoeck & Ruprecht, 1923).

G.N. Stanton, *A Gospel for a New People* (Edinburgh: T. & T. Clark, 1992).

B.H. Streeter, *The Four Gospels* (London: Macmillan, 1924).

The New Testament of our Lord and Saviour Jesus Christ, in the Original Greek, with Notes and Introductions, by Chr. Wordsworth, D.D. Bp. of Lincoln (London: Rivingtons, 7th edn, 1870).

3

MATTHEW'S WORLD

WHERE DO WE PLACE MATTHEW in the world of the first-century Mediterranean? The question is not simply a geographical one. It is also, and more answerably, a cultural historical one. Matthew's Gospel is without question a book of enormous significance in the development of the cultures of Europe. It stands at the parting of the ways between church and synagogue. It also marks a significant point in the development of the church into an institution with rules and formal organization. It would then be good to know as much as possible about its location and the subsequent history of its reception in the church. How much can we know?

Let us start with its origins. The difficulty, as with so many New Testament writings, is that we have very little, other than the Gospel itself, to go on. We need to pick up what clues we can in the Gospel itself. That is by general acknowledgment a difficult task even when one is dealing with the Epistles. They are at least mostly addressed to particular situations; on the other hand one hears only one side of the question. The Gospels by contrast are stories, ostensibly at least telling about events which precede the Evangelist's situation by some 50 years. How much then can we learn from Matthew's Gospel about the situation of his church?

J.L. Martyn, in a book which has been highly influential in Johannine studies, suggested that the stories of the Fourth Gospel have to be read on two levels: as referring both to particular events in Jesus' life and to Jesus' 'presence in actual events experienced by the Johannine church'. This is a useful proposal which works well in Martyn's case because he can find some clear pointers to the situation in the life of his community. A reference to 'being put out of the synagogue', such as we find in Jn 9.22, 12.42 and 16.2, may start off a whole train of inference which will cast light on the original setting of the Gospel. It is probably mostly true that good story-tellers shape their story in such a way as to resonate with their hearers' situation, but that does not mean that it is always easy to infer from the story what precisely that situation was.

There are in fact some clues, references in the telling of the story, which clearly reflect Matthew's situation rather than that of the stated situation in the life of Jesus.

Thus when Jesus refers to the church in 16.18 and 18.17 (the only two occurrences of the word in all the Gospels) we are clearly being transported from the world of Jesus' Galilean ministry to the life of the early Christian community.

Again, there are some tell-tale features associated with Matthew's presentation of Jesus' opponents. Matthew portrays the Pharisees as Jesus' main opponents. He often adds them into Mark's account (12.24, 38; 21.45; 22.34-35, 41). They are specifically targetted in 5.20 and 15.12-14 and they are the subject of a particularly fierce attack in ch. 23.

Furthermore the Pharisees are often paired with the Scribes (5.20; 12.38; 15.1; 23.2, 13, 14, 15, 23, 27, 29). This linking is specific to Matthew and may reflect a situation after 70 CE when there were only Pharisaic scribes.

Another interesting feature of Matthew's narrative is the coupling of the Pharisees and the chief priests in Mt. 21.45 (whereas Mark has previously referred to the chief priest and scribes and elders) and in 27.62 (the narrative, peculiar to Matthew, of the sealing of the tomb). This puts the Pharisees in a position of authority which they did not hold during Jesus' lifetime but did after 70. We have here a kind of double reference, on the one hand to the situation at the time of Jesus and on the other to that of Matthew's church.

Finally we might notice the way in which Matthew refers to 'their synagogues' on a number of occasions: 4.23; 9.35;

10.17; 12.9; 13.54. These are peculiar to Matthew where they occur, although the expression also occurs in Mk 1.23 and some textual traditions have a similar expression in Mk 1.21. Clearly such an expression reflects a separation between the narrator and the 'synagogue' which must tell us something about his stance. The same is also true of expressions like 'their scribes' (7.29), 'their cities' (11.1) and 'their country' (13.54).

Thus there are at least some indications that Matthew's Gospel was written in a situation where the church was in process of developing its structures and where there was a sense of both antagonism and separation between the Christian community and the Jewish community.

Matthew in the History of the Early Church

With these brief but not insignificant clues in mind let us turn first to consider Matthew's situation in the development of the early Christian community.

It has been said that the earliest history of the Christian church is almost impossible to reconstruct. What we have in the New Testament are merely fragments of a much larger canvas most of which we shall never be able to recover. The danger, if this is right, is that we then try to piece together the fragments which we have into a complete picture, with inevitable distortions. There is obviously truth in this, although we cannot of course know how much is missing. We should proceed with caution when constructing the larger picture.

What then can we say with some measure of confidence?

Christian Mission and the Hellenists
We know from Acts 6 that quite early on the church in Jerusalem, which played a very important role in the first generations of Christianity, experienced some kind of a division. The immediate cause was the difficulties experienced by the Hellenists in relation to the daily distribution of food to widows. The Hellenists, as opposed to the Hebrews, clearly felt that their widows were disadvantaged in the daily distribution. The upshot, according to Acts, is that there were appointed Seven to oversee the daily distribution.

So much we can read in Acts. We need to do some reading between the lines to pick out its meaning. First, who were the Hellenists and Hebrews? Martin Hengel ('Between Jesus and Paul') has suggested that the terms refer to different language groups within the early community, those who spoke Greek and those who spoke Hebrew or Aramaic. Among the former will have been those who had come to live in Jerusalem in their old age, and who may have felt excluded not only from the distribution of food but also, for linguistic reasons, at the meetings of the church for worship and prayer. It is also noticeable in Acts 6 that although the Seven are appointed to serve tables, their leader, Stephen, immediately appears as a powerful preacher who causes great anxiety among the Jewish leaders in Jerusalem because, they say, he speaks 'words against the holy place and the law'. (Acts 6.13) Thus it appears that the Seven were not merely 'deacons' with limited administrative tasks. Hengel believes that they were in fact the appointed leaders of a new Greek speaking group with its own meetings for worship and prayer. Once the group gains a measure of autonomy, they preach openly and publish their under-standing of Jesus' teaching which is said to be critical of the Law and the Temple. The immediate result is that this group of Christians is persecuted, Stephen is martyred and they flee to Antioch from where they continue to proclaim their version of Christianity. By contrast the Hebrews remain in Jerusalem and continue to worship in the Temple.

Wandering Charismatics and Urban Communities
This provides us with one early account of the way in which Christianity spread. The persecution of Christians in Jerusalem led to their scattering 'throughout the region of Judaea and Samaria'. (Acts 8.1) Acts adds 'except for the apostles'. This suggests a picture of the apostles ruling over the Jerusalem church while Christianity spread through the agency of those who had been persecuted. As G. Theissen has argued in *The First Followers of Jesus*, this picture is over-simplified. We have evidence from Paul's letters that not all the apostles were always to be found in Jerusalem. At his visit recorded in Gal. 1.18-19 he sees only Peter and James, the Lord's brother. Gal. 2.11 tells us of Peter's visit to

Antioch and of course there are many traditions of Peter's visit to and martyrdom in Rome. Rather than seeing Christianity as almost an accidentally missionary movement (though of course Luke records the mission charge to the disciples in Acts 1), Theissen has argued that we should see it as, in its early stages at least, a movement which is driven by 'wandering charismatics', those who are actively seeking a new mode of existence driven by a sense of the breakdown of the old order (social anomie). It is such people who are idealized by stories like the mission charge in Mk 6.7-13 and by passages like Mt. 6.25-34; 8.18-22; 10.1-42. Prophetic figures occur in Mt. 7.15; 10.41; 23.34, were still to be found in the church of the second century (*Didache* 11.4), and required the support of the local communities, something, as the *Didache* suggests, which could easily become a problem. There is, that is to say, room for tension here between those who are driven by the Spirit to a wandering, mendicant existence, proclaiming the Gospel, and those who seek to realise their Christian discipleship in small Christian communities, living a relatively stable existence. The latter group will soon begin to develop goals of its own, to seek ways of surviving as a community, of dealing with disputes, of distributing power and of working out its relationship with surrounding society.

Of course we have vivid evidence in Paul's letters of the tensions that could arise between such itinerant figures and the local churches. Paul is certainly someone caught up in the Spirit, driven to preach the Gospel to the Gentiles in the vivid expectation of the coming of the new age. Nevertheless his missionary activity may well originally have started at the behest of the church at Antioch (Acts 13.1-3). When, however, he loses the support of that church he can portray himself as a free apostle (1 Cor. 9.1-2), a claim based on his 'seeing the Lord' (1 Cor. 9.1; cf. Gal. 1.12). He has the right to food and support, but rarely makes use of it (1 Cor. 9), though this may cause his churches to question his trust in them. He proclaims a gospel free from the Law and finds himself sometimes in controversy with those of his converts who wish to give shape to their lives by appeal to the Law (Galatians). Nevertheless his letters are testimony to the need of his churches for advice and guidance on practical matters which threaten to divide the community. His authority which is based solely on his churches' recognition of him is challenged by other itinerant prophets who come with letters of recommendation from elsewhere (2 Cor. 3). His churches can all too easily be swayed by other itinerant preachers, just as he himself once swayed them. Paul, however, is deeply uneasy with any form of external authority, whether it be some form of official recognition or status, or some 'written code' (2 Cor. 3.6) of law, even, it might seem, of an appeal to the words and life of Jesus (2 Cor. 5.16). Nevertheless he too seeks recognition from Jerusalem and is anxious that the collection from his churches will be received by Jerusalem as a mark of such recognition (Rom. 15.30-31). And of course he appeals to the written 'Scriptures' and writes authoritative letters himself.

Thus we can see here clearly enough some of the issues which will increasingly engage the early Christian communities and their leaders, their prophets, teachers and evangelists. What claims to recognition and support do wandering prophets properly have? If they are not to be allowed to disturb the peace of the local community and if the community is to form its own judgment between their sometimes conflicting messages, then it must develop some canons of judgment of its own. But what sort of canons? Is the church which is led by the Spirit to return to the letter? Is the freedom of the Spirit which empowers prophets to preach the gospel to be restricted by the development of a local church leadership which is officially appointed and maintained? Does the church not need to develop appropriate codes of conduct in order to avoid suspicion and persecution? How far should it deviate from existing norms and patterns of behaviour? Some may have argued that in the light of the imminence of the end, such codes were now out of place, but as time went on the need to order the church's affairs grew. In all this the church is necessarily beginning to construct for itself a 'social world' which will enable it to live more or less at peace with its surrounding society. Such questions run through the writings of the New Testament. They have already left their mark on the writings and traditions which Matthew inherited.

Evidence of the Issue of Community Norms in Matthew's Sources

1. *Mark.* We have of course to be careful when we attempt to describe the way in which Matthew's sources were already addressing such questions. We should not simply assume that their authors or compilers are always addressing such issues directly. Mark may have had many reasons for compiling his Gospel, not the least of which may have been the simple desire to preserve the church's traditions about Jesus. Ernest Best (*Mark: The Gospel as Story*, pp. 51-54) has suggested that Mark writes primarily as a pastor, trying to reassure his congregation in the face of doubts and difficulties, by presenting to them a picture of Jesus as a caring pastor and shepherd of the church.

But of course the very fact of wanting to preserve the tradition indicates that Mark no longer expects the *imminent* end of the world (see Mk 13.10) and one may certainly ask whether his intention in recording the tradition is not also in a broad sense apologetic. Time and again, Mark refers to Jesus as a teacher, while recording relatively little of his teaching. Here is a new teaching 'with authority' (1.27). He certainly does on occasion speak very dismissively of the Law (7.19; 10.5), but for the most part, such issues are not directly engaged. The overall picture, however, is of a 'teacher' who is itinerant and whose closest associates are called to follow him in an itinerant ministry. In the end, it is the narrative itself which is Mark's great achievement. Is not the act of recording this life and death also a way of staking out a claim that this Jesus is the Son of God, that what is recorded here shall form the basis of a new view of the world? That is to say, the process of forging authoritative writings which can anchor the community, give it direction and stamp out a place for it in the ancient world has begun. We should, however, be wary of seeing too much direct engagement with the specific issues of itinerant prophets, of community norms and discipline.

2. *Q.* The collection of sayings on which Matthew and Luke drew, 'Q', is, of course, a more shadowy document, if document at all. One striking feature is the number of sayings

which exalt a life of radical discipleship: in Matthew's version, 6.25-33; 8.18-22; 10.7-16, 26-42. Here one feels the life of the itinerant preacher is being commended and upheld, a radical new way of life is being commended which breaks sharply with old rules and ways ('leave the dead to bury their dead'). Yet at the same time the collection contains sayings which strongly affirm the law and the teaching of Jesus as transcending the Law: 5.18, 39-42, 43-48; 7.12. Moreover, as a collection of Jesus' sayings and parables, Q is, as we have seen, analogous to other collections in the ancient world of the sayings of philosophers and wise men. So, again, there is a step being taken here, particularly if it is a written document, towards establishing the position and authority of Jesus the teacher. The emphasis on Jesus' teachings is, of course, all the more striking in Q, because of the absence of any miracle stories or passion narrative. However, it would be a mistake to think that Q simply presents Jesus as a philosopher-teacher; there is a strong sense of his imminent return as the Son of Man in power (24.26-28, 37-41), which one assumes is closely related to the ethos of radical discipleship which we have already noticed. Jesus' teaching is the announcement of the wisdom of God which presages the final revelation of his glory. The miracle of it is that it has been revealed to 'babes' (11.25-27). (There are some scholars who argue that there were different versions of Q, and that the predictions of the return of the Son of Man belong to the later editions. As we do not have any separate version of Q, it seems to me impossibly bold to speculate about different recensions.)

3. *Matthew's special traditions, M*. Finally, there is Matthew's own special material, which may or may not have been in written form. This contains material of different kinds: a genealogy, infancy narratives, parables, miracles and other narratives, sayings of Jesus. Strikingly, it contains much material about community affairs (16.17-19; 18.15-22; 23.8-11) which reflects a concern with order and discipline. It contains sayings which are strongly affirmative of the Law (5.17, 19-20) as well as sayings which affirm Jesus' transcendence of the Law (5.21-24, 27-32, 33-37, 38-42). It also contains a number of parables which deal with the subject of

judgment: 13.24-30, 36-43 (wheat and the tares); 13.47-50 (the dragnet); 25.1-13 (wise and foolish virgins); 25.31-46 (sheep and goats).

All of this is Matthew's immediate tradition. We know that he was familiar with it, that he took it over and dealt with the problems which it raised in his own way. We are on pretty firm ground here; not simply fitting pieces together because they are the only bits which we have. Summarizing, one might say that in Matthew's immediate tradition we can discern: 1. differing attitudes to the Law: some strongly affirmative, some critical, some dismissive; 2. differing attitudes to the eschaton, ranging from urgent expectation (Q), to the dimming of such expectations (Mark) and their parabolic reworking in Matthew's special material; 3. different presentations of Jesus, as miracle worker, teacher, as crucified and risen Lord; 4. some evidence that questions of institutional structures were becoming problematical.

Matthew's Community

Before we can ask how Matthew uses these given materials to provide a sense of direction to his community, a further question arises. In order to know how Matthew attempted to give direction to his community, we need to have some idea about the kind of community he was writing for and the situation in which it found itself. Where was it located geographically? Where is it to be placed in relation to developments in the early Church? Where did it stand in relation to Judaism?

The Geographical Location of Matthew's community
Scholars are divided as to where to locate Matthew geographically. There is general agreement that it comes from Syria: its Jewish character and its relation to Q would speak for this. Some favour Antioch, for the reasons that a large town like Antioch would make possible the rapid distribution of the Gospel that occurred, that there was a substantial settlement of Jews there, and that the Gospel is mentioned by Ignatius of Antioch shortly after the turn of the century. The first two points would be true of other Syrian cities, the third has some force.

There is also a good, indeed a prior question, raised by

Stanton (*Gospel for a New People*, pp. 50-51), about whether
we should speak of Matthew's 'community' at all. Was he
undertaking such a major work only for the sake of one
'house-church' or did he not from the start envisage a much
wider circulation and therefore write with general aims
rather than in order to meet quite specific needs of a particular group? It is probably right to say that the average
Christian group meeting for worship in a house in a
Hellenistic city would not have numbered more than 50 or so.
But then the Christian community in Antioch or some other
Syrian city might well have been made up of a number of
such groups who would presumably have had contacts among
each other, though quite possibly they had varied back-
grounds and may have seen things rather differently.
Hellenistic Christians in Antioch from the first persecution of
Stephen may subsequently have been joined by Jewish
Christians from Jerusalem after its fall. Other groups may
have been related to the communities which preserved the Q
traditions. Moreover this situation may well have been
repeated in a number of cities in the area, making Matthew's
community not untypical of his day. Any Gospel, that is to
say, which was written for a particular cluster of house-
churches in a Syrian city would probably have had appeal
outside its immediate milieu, even though (or indeed,
precisely because) it could be related to pressing issues of the
community to which it was originally addressed. Nor should
we assume too uncritically that Matthew was writing only
with his own community in mind. The different groups
within it may well have alerted him to the diversity of views
within the wider church and he may have intended that his
Gospel should speak to this wider grouping.

Place of Matthew's Community within Earliest Christianity
What can we say about the nature of this community and of
its placing in the development of early Christianity which we
sketched out briefly above? U. Luz has suggested persuasively that Matthew's community has a particular closeness
to the Q tradition (*Matthew 1–7*, pp. 65-66) and argues that
this can be seen from his treatment of the offices of prophet
and scribe in the community. References to prophets (23.34:

the exalted Lord sends prophets, sages and scribes to Israel; 10.41: on the reception of prophets in the community; cf. also 5.12; 23.37) and to false prophets (7.15-23; 24.10-12) suggest strongly that such prophets were known in Matthew's community and that moreover these were wandering prophets of the kind referred to in Q. It is true that, as Luz acknowledges, nearly all these references are taken from Q; but their number and distribution makes it reasonable to suppose that the topic was of concern to Matthew himself.

Matthew also inserts references into his traditional material about Christian scribes (13.52, cf. 8.19; 23.34 where Q had only prophets and wise men; cf. also 'their' scribes, 7.29). In neither case is it Matthew's intention to emphasize the position of the office within the community: 'one is your teacher' (23.8); the whole community has the power of loosing and binding (18.18). The intention is to see scribes as part of the community and equally to relativize the importance of the wandering charismatics. 'Matthew writes from the perspective of a sedentary community.' (*Matthew 1–7*, p. 66) In a similar vein, one might add that the radical ethos of Mt. 6.25-34 with its call for freedom from preoccupation with possessions is somewhat tempered in its closing verses: 'Seek first the kingdom of God and its righteousness and all these things will be added to you'. This is a call for the subordination of concern for daily needs to the demands of the gospel, rather than for radical freedom from them: the ethos of the itinerant mendicant is exchanged for the ethos of the urban Christian community.

One of the questions which this discussion raises is to what extent Matthew's church could be seen as a scribal community, some kind of 'school of Matthew', as K. Stendahl suggested. Evidence for this comes from the extensive use of the Old Testament in the Gospel and from the 'fulfilment quotations'. We shall consider these more fully below. Here we need only say that the point made above, namely that Matthew's intention is to integrate the scribes into his community, without however giving them a position of prominence, tells against Stendahl's view.

In sum: Matthew's community seems to be growing away from the earlier stage of Christianity where wandering, prophetic figures exercised power and influence over small gathered groups. It may never have been wholly dependent on such figures and may, with its close links to Judaism, have had members who exercised a teaching role within the community, not least in their attempts to relate the faith to the Hebrew Scriptures. For all that, Matthew does not wish to elevate such figures into a central position of power and authority. It is still the presence of Emmanuel with the community (1.23; cf. 28.20) which is the ultimate authority.

The Relation of Matthew's Community to Judaism

At least since the major work of W.D. Davies on Rabbinic Judaism and the Gospel of Matthew scholars have had to confront the question: how far did Matthew's community still see itself as part of the Jewish community, how far had it already parted company? That is to say, we may need to see Matthew and his community not only as part of the developing world of earliest Christianity but also as part of the Jewish world which was undergoing a process of re-formation after the catastrophe of the destruction of the Temple in 70 CE.

This is, of course, not a simple matter. The difficulties of constructing a picture of first-century Judaism are formidable. The Dead Sea Scrolls have shed light on some aspects of it, but the community which produced them was eccentric to mainstream Judaism. The main sources for our knowledge of the Pharisees were not compiled till the end of the second century. The Jewish historian Josephus (*Ant.* 18.11-25, cf. 13.171-73; *War* 2.119-66), who has to be read with care, speaks of different 'philosophies': Pharisees, Sadducees, Essenes and a 'fourth philosophy' the followers of Judas the Galilean, who were the forerunners of the Jewish freedom fighters at the time of the Jewish War. How sharply such groups were divided is, of course, a matter of debate. E.P. Sanders has strongly argued that we need to be more conscious of the broad base of 'common Judaism' before 70, with its central focus in the Temple cult. It was this which the majority of the people, both in Palestine and in the Diaspora, supported and which they were in the end prepared to die for and which in all likelihood held the various groups together. By the same token, once the Temple

was gone there was need for a radical reconstruction of the
Jewish community and its religion. After the disastrous first
Jewish War, a coalition of those groups which had survived,
associated with the town of Jamnia and the Pharisee
Johanan ben Zakkai, was gradually put together and took
responsibility for the construction of a new form of Judaism
without the Temple. Within this coalition the Pharisees, who
had already been actively concerned with developing forms of
purity laws outside the Temple, were increasingly
influential.

Again there are significant debates among historians about
the nature of this development. (A convenient discussion of
these is given by J. Andrew Overmann in *Matthew's Gospel
and Formative Judaism*.) The Rabbinic accounts of the events
after the Fall of Jerusalem suggest that the Roman authori-
ties empowered the Pharisees under Johanan ben Zakkai to
establish an academy at Jamnia, which regulated Jewish life
and worship. In practice the emergence of the Pharisees as
the dominant force in Judaism may have been more gradual,
a process accompanied by conflict and struggle.

Thus the development of Christianity as a distinct religious grouping with its own self-definition begins crucially at
a time when major changes are taking place within Judaism.
Moreover the picture is further complicated by the fact that
these two movements, which will in time become sharply distinct despite their common roots, for a time see themselves
as rival contenders for the future of Israel. In retrospect one
can also see that the Christian movement itself divides: there
is a form of Jewish Christianity which is both separate from
the main body of the Church and from Judaism itself and
which eventually quietly disappears from view. There is
Catholic Christianity which admits Gentiles to full member-
ship of the church without requiring them to submit to the
Jewish Law and which becomes dominant. The question
scholars have to consider is: where in all this does Matthew
stand?

Does Matthew's community still essentially see itself as
part of Israel, indeed the 'true Israel'? Was it written before
or after the Fall of Jerusalem? If after, did the community
see itself as in competition with the leaders of the Jewish

people around the coalition of Jamnia? Or does it already
stand on the other side of the parting of Christianity and
Judaism, regarding itself as part of a new community which
is separate and distinct from the Jewish people (as for
instance Paul sees his churches as distinct from Israel)? Or
was Matthew not a Jew at all, as some have suggested, nor
particularly interested in the controversies which troubled
Jewish Christian communities at their inception?

It is important here to realize that the answers to such
questions depend on careful and detailed work on the text of
the Gospel. We have no independent, external evidence:
there are no other first-century documents which would give
us the answers to such questions. We have to look at the way
Matthew works with his traditional material, reworking
Mark's narrative and incorporating large amounts of
teaching material, all the time modifying and putting his
own particular interpretation upon it. However in a short
study guide we shall be able to do no more than give the
outline of such arguments.

First, U. Luz in his commentary (*Matthew 1–7*, pp. 79-82)
has made a strong case for the Jewishness of Matthew, based
on the Jewishness of Matthew's language and style of composition. Against this need to be set the claims that the anti-
Jewishness of Matthew is so strong that it could not have
been written by a Jew; that he supported the Gentile mission
and that he avoids Aramaic words. I think Luz's case is the
more telling. People may have all sorts of views, though
being of the same ethnic origin; it is almost, though not
quite, impossible to shake off inherited linguistic characteristics. Avoiding the use of words in another language is of
course a matter over which one does have control.

Secondly, I think that it is wholly unlikely that Matthew
was written before 70. Mark's Gospel cannot be any earlier
than the later part of the 60s and if as is highly probable,
Matthew used Mark, then this simply would not allow
enough time for the dissemination of Mark's work and for
Matthew's redaction of it.

It is much more difficult to know on which side of the parting of the ways between Judaism and Christianity to place

Matthew's Gospel. There are elements in the Gospel which
seem to indicate a living connection with Judaism. The disciples who are sent out in ch. 10 are told to go only 'to the lost
sheep of the house of Israel'. Matthew includes the story
about the Temple tax (17.24-27) which would seem to be of
doubtful interest to those who have parted company with
Judaism altogether. Perhaps most tellingly in Mt. 23.2-3 we
read: 'the scribes and Pharisees sit on Moses' seat; so practise and observe whatever they tell you, but not what they
do; for they preach but do not practise'. This certainly seems
to read much more convincingly as a recognition by people
within Israel of the *de facto* position of power which the
scribes and Pharisees hold in their community, *which power
is therefore to be acknowledged*, than as an outsider's
statement. It is hard to see how Matthew could have let
something like this stand if his community had just parted
company with the Jewish community precisely over questions which included importantly matters of interpretation of
the Law.

There are, on the other hand, powerful arguments which
suggest that the community stands on the other side of the
parting of the ways. G. Stanton (*Gospel for a New People*,
pp. 124-31) has put these clearly and argued for this position extensively throughout his book. He gives five main
reasons:

1. the sustained attack, often in passages which are
    clearly Matthew's redactional work, against scribes
    and Pharisees;
2. the association of the scribes and Pharisees with the
    synagogue (often referred to in redactional phrases,
    'you' or 'their' synagogues);
3. the clear distinction Matthew makes between church
    and synagogue, where the church has its own
    entrance rite and liturgical practice and where the
    presence of Jesus with the church supersedes the
    presence of God in the Temple;
4. passages which speak about the 'transference' of the
    kingdom to a new people who will include Gentiles:
    8.5-13; 15.13 and Stanton's prime witness, 21.41 and
    43: 'Therefore I tell you, the kingdom of God will be

taken away from you and given to a people who will produce the proper fruit';

5.   in 28.15 Matthew addresses his readers directly and refers to the 'Jews' with their rival account of the resurrection as a group separate from the church.

Needless to say there are counters which can be made to some of these points.

1.   Stanton himself has said that conflicts tend to be fiercest between those who are closely linked together, and one could find sufficient parallels in the literature of Jewish sectarianism for Matthew's attacks on the scribes and Pharisees.

2.   Matthew's references to 'their' synagogues may be distinguishing different assemblies within Judaism.

3.   The development of a church with its own forms of organization and structures, in some sense parallel to those of the other forms of Judaism, could be a development located either in or outside of Judaism. Nevertheless, Stanton's point about the presence of Jesus in the church remains a powerful one.

4.   Nor are the passages about the 'transference' of the kingdom easily dismissed. One might, however, ask when this transference is to occur. The parable of the vineyard in 21.33-41 might suggest that the removal of the kingdom is the direct result of the crucifixion of Jesus and therefore takes place immediately. On the other hand, Luz (*Matthew 1-7*, pp. 84-85) has suggested that Matthew's community saw the destruction of Jerusalem as the judgment of God on the Jewish people for their rejection of the Christian mission. Even this is presumably a restrospective judgement. Passages like Matthew 23 suggest dialogue and conflict with the leaders of Judaism for some time after the destruction of the Temple.

The issue here is, I think, delicately balanced, though Stanton finds the view that the Gospel was written before the parting of the ways 'implausible' (*Gospel for a New People*, p. 124). Perhaps part of the problem lies in defining the parting of the ways. When Qumran vilified the Temple

hierarchy and decreed that only those who had taken the
oath of the community were sons of the covenant, they had
obviously parted company with the Temple priesthood in a
significant sense. Yet in another sense they still saw themselves as the faithful remnant of Israel. In this sense they
can be properly described as a sect, living within the wider
community, yet vilifying its leadership. Did Matthew's
community go through such a stage before it eventually
ceased to see itself as part of the wider community at all, and
instead attached itself to the (majority?) church which had
broken with the Law over the non-circumcision of Gentiles?
It is interesting that Stanton can compare Matthew's polemic
against the Pharisees with the similar polemic against them
in the Damascus Document of the Qumran community as
both instances of a minority community distancing itself
from the parent body (see esp. p. 96). But that is of course
precisely a move made by those who have not yet fully *parted
company* with the parent body.

Luz has suggested that the Gospel is written at a 'turning
point' (*Matthew 1–7*, p. 84) in the life of the community
which is constituted by the decision whether or not to engage
in the Gentile mission. He sees Matthew as an advocate of
the Gentile mission, but recognizes that there are still vital
issues which will not have been clarified by his Gospel,
namely the extent to which those engaged on the mission
would then be free to modify the Law. Thus for him too it
seems that the vital step is being proposed which will lead to
the separation of the two communities; but that even so not
all the ties have yet been cut. The process of parting,
whether more or less painful (Stendahl speaks of 'a far
smoother transition from Judaism to Christianity than we
usually suppose', *School of Matthew*, pp. xiii-xiv), was
certainly not such that it is easy to say exactly when the
transition occurred. I think, however, that there is no reasonable doubt but that by the time of the composition of
Matthew's Gospel the writing was, in a manner of speaking,
on the wall.

Matthew's Formation of his Community

At this point we can now ask what part Matthew intended
his Gospel to have in the development of his community.

What contribution did he expect it to make to the internal problems that the community was facing: the interaction between different styles of leadership, the need for clearer definition of roles within the group, the need for some form of disciplinary procedures? And what contribution to the crisis which was precipitated by the imminent or actual parting of the ways with Judaism: the need for redefining the boundaries and markers of the community once it had left the matrix of Judaism, indeed for defining the beliefs and rituals of the new community? It is unlikely that Matthew would have posed the questions in that sort of way; or that he would have separated the tasks out as neatly as that. He would have been aware, presumably, of the community's needs at different levels and must have had some overall strategy in writing his Gospel, but he would have also, to some extent, been forced by the nature of his work in redacting traditional material to respond *ad hoc* to themes and issues as they were raised by the material with which he was working. We should not moreover assume that his only purpose in writing the Gospel was to deal with issues of community building: he may, as Luz has suggested, have been equally interested in rekindling the flame of Christian faith and devotion. But again such matters are not wholly unrelated. Lastly, we need to remind ourselves that Matthew's community, in seeking to give clearer definition to its organization and world-view, is engaged in the same task as other forms of post-70 Judaism. It may not just have been in conflict with Judaism but it may also have been taking a few leaves from its book about how to achieve such ends.

These kinds of questions gain added sharpness when they are seen through the lens of sociological studies of the development of religious groups. They have only fairly recently been raised in such form in New Testament studies and work is therefore at a fairly preliminary stage. One useful book which has drawn together a lot of the relevant material is J. Andrew Overman's *Matthew's Gospel and Formative Judaism*. This along with the discussion in Stanton's *Gospel for a New People*, ch.4, gives a fuller introduction to the theoretical issues which such study raises.

1. *Scripture and Law*. For Jews God's purposes and will for his people had been revealed in Torah, in Scripture. Any new or reconstructed community which wanted to claim continuity with Israel would have to show where it stood in relation to Scripture. This would mean on the one hand providing scriptural, that is traditional, support for what one was actually doing; and also showing how the new elements that one wanted to introduce, or had introduced, related to the Law.

The first thing to notice is that there is a considerable difference between the way in which Matthew went about providing scriptural legitimation for his community and that in which 'Jamnian' Judaism did. Whereas Matthew principally tells a story, though one which includes a substantial amount of discourse material, Johanan ben Zakkai and his group set about collecting together the sayings of the scribes and the Wise men, which would provide the substance of the new interpretation of the Law and eventually find their way into the Mishnah and Talmud. This is not to say that the followers of Johanan ben Zakkai stopped telling stories but that the principal product of their efforts to reshape Judaism was comprised predominantly of sayings.

One of the important features of Matthew's use of narrative is to set the story of Christ and the church within a wider historical context going back to Abraham and revealing the continuing purposes of God for his people. In the telling of that story, however, there is room for showing how it is anchored to Scripture, for showing Jesus as interpreting the Law and expounding his own authoritative teachings as its fulfilment. In both of these contexts the notion of 'fulfilment' is central.

a. *Scriptural quotations*. Matthew's concern to show how the Christian story is rooted in Scripture is evidenced by the frequency of its citation and of the allusions to it in his Gospel. He has all of Mark's quotations and allusions and all the Q references, as well as a substantial number of references of his own. One of the features of the Gospel that has attracted particular attention is the 'fulfilment quotations', quotations which are introduced by a formula including the words: 'in order that what was spoken by the prophet...might be fulfilled': 1.22-23; 2.15, 17-18, 23; 4.14-16; 8.17; 12.17-21; 13.35; 21.4-5; 27.9-10. There are some difficult issues raised by these quotations. What text is being used: the Hebrew Bible or the Greek translation, the Septuagint? There is certainly a marked divergence in many cases from the Greek translation which Matthew otherwise seems to favour when citing Scripture. Were these 'fulfilment' quotations sought out by Matthew himself or was he using a collection put together by group of scribes within his own church?

These are technical questions. A number of points can be made. There is no agreement between scholars as to whether or not Matthew was responsible for the choice of Scriptural quotations. Many, including Luz (*Matthew 1-7*, pp. 156-63), favour the view that the fulfilment quotations, which have a rather distinctive form of text as opposed to the rest of Matthew's quotations, come from some kind of scribal activity within his community. Stanton (*Gospel for a New People*, pp. 358-59) who questions Matthew's dependence on the Septuagint for his biblical text outside the 'fulfilment quotations', suggests that he may well have been responsible for at least some of them. Certainly the formula itself can be seen as arising out of Matthew's redaction of Mk 14.49 and if Matthew has composed the formula may he not be responsible for the quotations too?

The form of the quotations is important, too. They are not words of Scripture put into any of the characters' mouths (though Matthew can do this, cf. Mt. 9.13) but rather words addressed by the narrator to his readers. As such they may give us an important indication of Matthew's purpose. R.E. Brown has written: 'these citations emphasize that the whole of Jesus' life, down to the last detail, lay within God's foreordained plan' (cited by Overman, *Matthew's Gospel*, p. 74). Their purpose is not simply to anchor the events of Jesus' life in history (to prove that it happened), but to show that it was part of God's saving purpose for his people. However, the quotations, which are unevenly distributed through the Gospel, seem to do more than just that. They underline central themes of Matthew's work: Jesus is God with us, the presence of God in the world (1.23); he is the shepherd of his people (2.6); God's Son (2.15).

Matthew's use of Scripture here has sometimes been compared to the form of scriptural interpretation found at
Qumran, known as pesher. In the Qumran pesher on
Habakkuk, for instance, the reader is taken through the text
verse by verse, each verse being shown to refer to some event
of significance in the life of the community. Matthew's procedure is in one sense clearly different. He does not follow the
text of a particular book, but rather chooses his quotations
widely. Nevertheless the comparison is interesting. Just as
Qumran was a community seeking reassurance that its
chosen path was in continuity with God's will, so too
Matthew's. Overman has suggested that what is going on
here is part of a struggle *within Judaism* for legitimacy;
Matthew's church had yet to part from Judaism. Possibly,
but even if Matthew's community had already left the Jewish
fold, it would still need powerful traditional forms of
legitimation, indeed arguably would need them even more.
The point is that both Judaism and Matthew's community
orientate themselves by 'Scripture' and will continue to
struggle over the interpretation of Scripture whatever their
relationship to each other.

b. *Interpretation of the Law*. The question of the correct
interpretation of the Law is raised sharply in a number of
stories in the Gospel which scholars define as 'conflict
stories', stories, that is, where Jesus is engaged in dispute by
opponents, often enough the scribes and the Pharisees.
Matthew shows his interest in such conflicts by creating
three more conflict stories additional to the ones he has
found in that form in his sources: Mt. 12.38-42; 22.34-40;
22.41-46 (so Overman, *Matthew's Gospel*, pp. 78-86). Not all
of these stories are directly concerned with law in the sense
of rules of conduct; some are, some address broader matters
of theology and faith.

I shall discuss one which Matthew already found as a conflict story, the dispute about purity in Mt. 15.1-20, taken
from Mark 7. Matthew has made a number of significant
changes to his source. In the first place he has reshaped the
first part of the story. In Mark 'the Pharisees and some of the
scribes' ask Jesus why his disciples eat with unwashed
hands, thus breaking the tradition of the elders. Jesus

responds by quoting Isa. 29.13 which accuses them of teaching 'as doctrines human precepts'. There then follows a section in which Jesus in turn accuses them of breaking the Law in the practice of Corban (declaring something owed to one's parents a sacrificial gift and therefore withholding it). Matthew has changed the order; he has Jesus challenge the Pharisees over the tradition of the elders by confronting them immediately with the practice of Corban, and then deliver the saying from Isaiah as a conclusion to the encounter.

This section is followed in Mark immediately by a further saying by Jesus on the subject of purity, addressed first to the crowd and then explained to his disciples by Jesus. Matthew interposes between the saying to the crowd and the explanation to the disciples a section in which Jesus attacks the Pharisees as blind guides and a 'planting' not from his Father which will be torn out (vv. 12-14). Three other changes to this section need to be noticed: first Matthew reformulates Jesus' saying to the crowds about purity. Whereas Mark's form: 'there is nothing outside a person that by going in can defile; but the things that come out are what defile' makes a general distinction between what is outside and what is inside, Matthew's version: 'it is not what goes into the mouth that defiles a man, but it is what comes out of the mouth that defiles', omits this distinction and focuses strictly on what goes into the mouth. Secondly, Matthew omits Mark's editorial comment in 7.19, 'thus he declared all foods clean.' Thirdly, he discusses impurity in terms of what comes out of the mouth, meaning from the heart, and changes Mark's list of such terms to bring it much closer into line with the ten commandments.

Two things are striking here: one is the way in which Matthew has heightened the polemic against the Pharisees. He refers to them in terms which, as Stanton has pointed out, are reminiscent of Qumran's polemic against the Pharisees (*Gospel for a New People*, p. 96: 'blind guides', CD 1.9). The second is the way he has withdrawn from Mark's wholesale rejection of food laws and instead emphasized the commitment of his community to the weightier matters of the Law. I think Overman is mistaken here to think that Matthew is

attempting to argue that 'Jesus and the disciples do not play
fast and loose with the law *or the Pharisaic paradosis*'
(*Matthew's Gospel*, p. 83, my italics). On the contrary he is
arguing that the Pharisaic traditions break the Law (possibly
identifying the whole people of Israel with this practice: this
people honours me with their lips...teaching', whereas the
practice of eating with unwashed hands (*not*, as Mark would
have it, eating unclean foods) is properly in accordance with
the Law, so at least Matthew's summary at the end of the
section.

What precisely is going on here? Is Matthew simply
conducting a battle against the Pharisees *at a distance*, now
that the separation has occurred between the two communities? Or is this part of Matthew's struggle, albeit from
outside the synagogue, against the Pharisees' attempt to
make their understanding of Torah normative for the whole
of Judaism? But then we might ask whether Matthew would
have been interested in conducting such a struggle if he had
already parted company with Judaism and was arguing
instead for the Gentile mission. Again we need perhaps to
say that the process of parting is not a sudden one and that
the battles being fought out here are still ones which matter
to Matthew, whether because he still hopes to bring Judaism
round to his way of thinking, against the Pharisees; or
whether because he is here using the Pharisees as a foil by
which to bring home to his community—and the wider
Gentile church which he is correcting here—that there is no
conflict between the Law as such and Jesus' and the
Church's teaching. In the latter case his position would be
not unlike that of Paul's Galatian congregation who turn to
the Law (as John Barclay has suggested in *Obeying the
Truth*, pp. 68-72), because they need some such strong
ethical tradition to anchor themselves and to enable them to
consolidate their community once they have broken away
from their former paganism. Here Matthew, of course, is not
looking for a new source of authority but rather fighting both
against Pharisaic counter-charges and against anti-Torah
elements in his own tradition.

2. *Community Norms and Discipline*. Whether or
not Matthew was writing from inside or outside the Jewish

community, he was engaged in consolidating and legitimising
his community. There were inherited problems arising out of
the development of forms of Christian ministry in the
earliest days; there were problems which came with the
growth of sedentary communities; there were problems
which arose out of the heightened tension and conflict
between his community and the Jewish leadership. How
Matthew set about dealing with all this was, as we have said,
partly by detailed editing of his traditional material (as we
saw when looking at the section on purity in Mt. 15.1-20),
partly by constructing large blocks of material, which would
give shape and sense to the Gospel as a whole. In particular
he constructed five large discourses, and a subordinate
one (ch. 23), in which the majority of Jesus' teaching is
contained. In these sections the foundations are laid for a
new community: a new social world is being created.
Whether Matthew specifically intended his readers to draw a
connection between his five major discourses and the five
books of the Pentateuch may be disputed; but he was
claiming that his community had a substantial body of
teaching which had been revealed by God. In a somewhat
similar way the Rabbis would at the end of the next century
produce the Mishnah, their compilation of teaching which
too was claimed to have its origins in divine revelation. We
shall not be able to deal with all these discourses. Instead we
shall look at the Sermon on the Mount which is the fullest
exposition of community norms and ch. 18 which deals
explicitly with matters of community discipline.

a. *The Sermon on the Mount*. Matthew's Sermon on the
Mount is based on a collection of sayings which existed in Q
and of which we find a much shorter form in Lk. 6.20-49.
Matthew has largely followed the order of Q but has
considerably expanded it by the addition of sayings from
elsewhere in Q and from his own special material.

Its structure is not easy to identify clearly. There are
certain patterns which appear to emerge obviously. 5.17,
which forms the opening of the main section of teaching after
the beatitudes is picked up again in 7.12 and so brackets the
main section, which is preceded by an introduction and
followed by a concluding passage which principally sets out

the two ways between which a disciple has to choose. The
form of the first half of the central section is clear too: there
are six 'antitheses' (about murder, adultery, divorce, oaths,
retaliation, love of enemies), i.e. passages where Jesus'
understanding of the Law is related to and contrasted with
the teaching of, largely at least, the Scriptures. Thereafter
things are less clear, though one thing is obvious, namely the
importance in what follows of the Lord's prayer in 6.9-13.
Bornkamm ('Der Aufbau der Bergpredigt', *NTS* 24
[1977–78], pp. 419-32) has suggested that what follows the
Prayer is a commentary on it. This may be too specific a
proposal but what it shows is the extent to which the values
in the Prayer correspond to the injunctions which are then
subsequently given to the disciples. Luz (*Matthew 1–7*,
pp. 211-13) sees the Prayer as the central pivot of the
Sermon as a whole.

Two points emerge from this: that Matthew has taken
great care over his construction of ths passage, and that
there is not just ethical instruction in the Sermon but
instruction in worship and prayer. What we have here is not
just a set of rules but the foundation document of a new religious community which sees itself as children of a heavenly
father who will forgive and reward the 'righteous' (5.6, 10,
20, 45; 6.1, 33), those who are faithful to him and his Son's
commands.

This interweaving of religious imagery with ethical
instruction is of vital importance in the construction of a new
community. It is not enough to lay down rules. As Peter
Berger has argued, a religious community needs to know
itself protected under a 'sacred canopy', living in a world
which is as it were shaped and held together by the source of
all reality. It is therefore striking that Matthew has almost
certainly himself added the phrase 'as in heaven so on earth'
in 6.10 and that the same motif is to be found in 5.45 where
love of enemies is enjoined 'so that you may be sons of your
father in heaven', and in 5.48 where the disciples are told to
'be perfect as your heavenly father is perfect'.

What then are the values which Matthew commends to
his community? The term which occurs throughout
the Gospel and at significant stages in the Sermon itself is

'righteousness' (7 times in the Gospel; the adjective 'righteous' occurs 17 times). Those who hunger and thirst after righteousness will be filled (5.6); to those who are persecuted for righteousness' sake belongs the kingdom of heaven (5.10); the disciples' righteousness is to exceed that of the scribes and Pharisees (5.20); the disciples are not to 'do their righteousness' ostentatiously (6.1); they are to seek first the kingdom of God and his righteousness (6.33). It is important to realize how different this use is from that of Paul who contrasts righteousness by 'works of the law' with righteousness which comes from faith. Here Matthew is quite clear about the connection between righteousness and works, as the saying in the context of warnings against false prophets makes clear: 'By their fruits you shall know them.' It is 'not everyone who says "Lord, Lord" who will enter into the kingdom of heaven but the one who does the will of my Father who is in heaven' (7.20-21). Such an emphasis means that Matthew remains firmly in the tradition of the Hebrew Scriptures which sees the Law as being there to provide guidance for God's people in the practical affairs of life. It is God's gift of guidance to his people and it is there to be done. Blessedness results from its performance, as well as from its study and from mediation on it. The righteous person is the one who sets his or her heart on doing the law and who indeed does it, as opposed to the sinner who does not.

But then what exactly is Matthew's community being enjoined to do? Is it simply to keep the Law? Is it to keep a new Law promulgated by Jesus on the Mountain to replace the Mosaic law? Or is it to keep the Law as definitively interpreted by Jesus? The difficulty here is this: if Matthew was suggesting that Jesus was proclaiming the definitive understanding of the Law, then one would expect him to be much more concerned to show how Jesus' interpretation differed from that of his contemporaries, notably of course the Pharisees (in 23.3 the disciples are even commanded to observe the teaching of the Pharisees!). If he was wanting to suggest that Jesus replaced the Law with a new Law then we would expect a much sharper distinction between the provisions of the old and of the new. We would not expect such strong affirmations of the continuing validity of the Law and the prophets.

The point can be made most clearly in relation to the antitheses which form the larger part of ch. 5. Here Jesus contrasts his teaching with what has been 'said of old'. This, of course, is not a bad thing. What is 'of old' is hallowed by tradition; the passive form 'is said' is probably a *passivum divinum*, that is to say a passive form which avoids the use of the divine name but which implies that it is God who has acted. Such 'contrasts' do not necessarily imply a contradiction between what was said in Scripture and what is now said by the teacher. Similar forms can be found in Rabbinic traditions to introduce the teaching of the sages on disputed verses of Scripture (Luz, *Matthew 1–7*, p. 276).

What contrast is then implied between that which was said of old and Jesus' teaching? There seem to be a number of different kinds of comparisons being made. In the case of the sayings about murder and adultery (5.21-26, 27-30), there seems to be a simple extension of the Law to embrace thoughts and desires as well as specific actions. Here one might say that the Law is being deepened, though it is true that it is also being made a lot less enforceable. In the case of the sayings about oaths and retaliation (5.33-37, 38-42) we might say that there is a similar extension of the intention of the old law. Here the old laws had been intended to limit swearing and the taking of vengeance. Jesus proposes that it should stop altogether. What is interesting by contrast with the previous cases is that here something which was permitted in the old law is now being forbidden. The intensification of the Law leads to its replacement by a new, more radical law. The saying about divorce (5.31-32) is altogether more difficult. Were it not for the exception for adultery we might have a case very similar to that of oaths and retaliation. The Law limits the freedom of men simply to cast their wives out: there must be a 'cause of offence' and he must give her a bill of divorce. Jesus extends this by forbidding divorce and declaring divorce to be another form of adultery. If Matthew had used the form of the saying as we have it in Lk. 16.18, then that is what we should have. But he, or his community before him, added the 'exception'. Now the saying reads like a contribution to the contemporary Pharisaic debates about what might constitute a 'cause of offence'. One school, the school of Hillel, ruled that anything that displeased the husband could constitute grounds for divorce; the other, that of Shammai, that only adultery could count *(Gittin* 9.10). In this sense Jesus is here presented as entering into contemporary debate and taking sides, rather than distancing himself from Pharisaic positions altogether.

Finally, Jesus commands love of enemies rather than love of neighbour and hatred of enemies (5.43-48). There is, however, no Scriptural base for hatred of enemies, at least not in the form of an explicit command. There are plenty of examples of it, a good number of which have divine sanction (e.g. Ps. 137.9; Josh. 10.12-14). Such explicit commands can be found in the Qumran literature (1 QS 1.10-11; 9.21-22; cf. 10.17-18) though even here it is fairly clear that hatred for enemies is not to be converted into action.

The Qumran community had disappeared by Matthew's time but its influence will not have vanished altogether. So this may be another example where Jesus is confronting contemporary interpretations of the Law. In that case here he is rejecting such interpretations: at the same time he is proposing his own interpretation which goes beyond the sense of the Levitical command (Lev. 19.18). For what he now proposes is not the intensification of love for one's neighbour, as in loving him or her not merely in explicitly commanded deeds, but in one's thoughts and motives. In fact, interestingly, Matthew omits here the Levitical phrase 'as yourself'. Rather what is commanded is the extension of the same love to another group, namely those who are antagonistic to the group itself. This is a radicalization of tendencies which are to be found certainly in the older Scriptures but which are nowhere so explicitly or boldly stated. What is being commanded here is moreover an imitation of God, such that the disciples may become his children. It is in such open generosity that divine and therefore human perfection lies (5.48; cf. Mt. 19.21). Is there a deliberate contrasting here with the Levitical command to be holy as I am holy (Lev. 19.2) with its implications of separation from all that is alien to God (cf. Lev. 20.26)?

What this discussion suggests is that there is a studied ambiguity about the way that Matthew is presenting the relation of Jesus' teaching to the Law. Alternatively one might say that there are reflected in the Sermon on the Mount some of the different attitudes to the Law which the community had evinced over the period in which it had moved ever closer to a complete break with Judaism. What his readers would have taken from it is clear, I think. They would have seen it as a clear legitimization of the community's way of life, over against the direction in which the Pharisees and their allies were trying to take Judaism.

b. *Matthew 18 and community discipline.* We need to say something more briefly about the way in which Matthew dealt with specific problems of discipline in his community. We have already noticed that there were tensions which might arise from the existence within the community of scribes and prophets with different claims to a hearing, particularly if the prophets saw themselves as having special authority which required them to answer to no one but God. We have already seen above how Matthew integrates the scribes into his own community. Where prophets are concerned, he is quick to warn against false prophets, and sets out clear criteria by which they are to be judged. They are to be judged by their conformity to the community norms (7.15-23). The language is admittedly graphic rather than specific. What are the 'ravenous wolves' doing? Presumably not making peace as children of God should (5.9). But Matthew may have had to face other problems which came partly from the simple fact of trying to institute some kind of internal disciplinary procedures in a community which had none, partly from the fact that his community was a very non-hierarchical one, which treated all members as brothers and was opposed to ranks and titles within it (23.8-12 which may well indicate that there were people in the community, perhaps not uninfluenced by the Pharisees, who saw this as the way to develop some system of authority.) There is also a further problem which is clearly indicated by ch. 18. The community was not only an egalitarian community; it was a community based on a principle of forgiveness which made it difficult to discipline people.

Matthew 18 is a chapter which provides some guidance in such a situation, though by no means all of it is simply practical guidance. A good deal of it is moral or theological exhortation. Thus it is probably a mistake to see it as a community rule, distinct in that respect from the other discourses in the Gospel. It certainly includes specific rulings on discipline (vv. 15-18), but it is also, like the Sermon on the Mount, a source of general ethical guidance.

The chapter starts with a section on the notion of greatness in the kingdom of heaven (vv. 1-5). True greatness consists in humility. Here Matthew takes a section from Mk 9.33-37 and reworks it. In Mark the disciples argue among themselves about which of them is greatest. In Matthew the question has been widened into a general question about status and position within the community: 'Who is the greatest in the *kingdom of heaven*?' Again Matthew adds his own interpretation to Jesus' action with the child by underscoring the child's lowliness. The Greek word has two meanings, either the virtue of humility or the humility of affliction (Ambrose). Commentators are divided over whether what is meant here is the virtue or simply the lowliness or powerlessness of the child. This is a slightly odd debate: the point of the injunction is that those in the Kingdom should acknowledge their smallness in the face of God: and such acknowledgment—theological or religious humility—can properly be seen as underpinning moral humility: not thinking of ourselves more highly than we ought to think. The whole section provides an interesting reworking of the opening of the Sermon on the Mount. The question of greatness is not unrelated to the question of the enjoyment of the blessings of the Kingdom. The exhortation to humility is close to the beatitudes to the poor in spirit and the meek. It sets out, as Trilling suggests (*Das wahre Israel*, p. 113), the broad theological perspective which informs the sayings about the little ones, about community discipline and about forgiveness in the rest of the chapter.

The chapter moves on in vv. 6-10 to consider the question of 'little ones'. The identity of the little ones is not clear but one possibility is that they were the poorer members of urban churches. Precisely who is causing them to stumble is also

not clear. The principle invoked is however evident: it is
better that those who cause such people to stumble should be
cut out of the community, than that the community should
suffer. Here again Matthew is following Mark (9.42-48), but
he changes Mark's section which talks metaphorically about
the need for self-discipline into a section about the need for
community discipline and exclusion.

This is however balanced by the particular slant which
Matthew gives to the parable of the shepherd and the sheep
(vv. 12-14). Here he is using a story from the common tradition he shares with Luke. Whereas Luke refers to the 'lost'
sheep (Lk. 15.4) and explains the parable in terms of repentance (v. 7), Matthew speaks about the sheep 'going astray'
(Mt. 18.12) and explains the parable in terms of 'not being
lost' (v. 14). Luke's parable is about bringing those outside
the group in; Matthew's about the need to do all in one's
power to ensure that the erring member is not finally lost to
the group. Matthew's concern here is clearly that of the
pastor who is seeking all means in his power to hold his
congregation together.

What we have had so far, however, has been in the nature
of general injunctions, using and modifying material which
already existed in the community's traditions. What comes
next, 18.15-20, is both more specific and also more original.
18.15-17 proposes procedures for dealing with recalcitrant
members of the community. If there is a dispute this should
be settled, if possible, between the two persons concerned.
Beyond that a small group should attempt to mediate; if that
fails, then the congregation as a whole should be brought in
and, if necessary, the offending party should be excluded.
The section probably bears some relation to the similar
section in Lk. 17.3-4, but has been substantially developed,
possibly in Matthew's own tradition. The meeting with one or
two others probably is intended first as a means of winning
the brother back, but it may also function as a form of legal
procedure, insuring that there are adequate witnesses if it
should come to more formal proceedings in front of the
congregation. The model here is clearly an Old Testament
one, as the reference to Deut. 19.15 makes clear. The climax
of the procedure is the congregation's decision which may

lead to the exclusion: 'let him be to you as a Gentile and a tax-collector'. In the context of a chapter which stresses the need to search for the one stray sheep and contains the injunction to forgive seventy times seven times, this can only be a painful acknowledgment of the realities of community life and of the need to have some way of drawing the line. Matthew invokes the authority which is given to the congregation of 'loosing and binding' (Mt. 16.19). This is a phrase which occurs regularly in later rabbinic writings where it may refer to the teaching authority of the rabbinate. Here it is more likely to be intended in a strictly disciplinary sense. Overman (*Matthew's Gospel*, p. 105) has drawn attention to parallel usage in the contemporary Jewish writer Josephus who talks about the Pharisees in the reign of Alexander Jannaeus having power 'to banish and recall, to loose and bind whomever they would' (*War* 1.111-16).

This exercise of the congregation's authority is then linked to the power of the congregation in prayer, itself linked to the presence of Jesus with them (Mt. 18, 19–20). The power to exclude, terrible though it is, should not be seen as the sole or indeed the principal power given to the congregation. Its principal function is to pray for the needs of the community. Moreover in so doing it will be reminded that its authority is not simply devolved to it, so that it, as it were, exercises it independently; it is rather power which comes from the living presence of the Lord with them.

Two final points may be made about this section. As Overman has pointed out, the congregation's action in loosing and binding will be confirmed in heaven. 'The actions and decisions of the community carry the force and authority of heaven' (*Matthew's Gospel*, p. 104). The same can be seen elsewhere in Matthew's Gospel (5.48; 6.10; 12.32; 16.19). The community reflects the order and values of the heavenly kingdom. 'In their power to bind and to loose, the Matthaean community represents a "mimetic reiteration" of the power and authority of the kingdom of heaven...In sociological terms the social nomos and the universal cosmos appear as coextensive' (*Matthew's Gospel*, p. 104).

The other point to notice is the emphasis placed throughout the chapter on forgiveness. In a sense the

problems of community discipline and control are exacer-
bated by the community's focus on forgiveness as a funda-
mental value. How can you take tough decisions and
discipline people if you teach that it is one's duty to go on and
on forgiving? The two parables in the chapter both attempt
to elucidate the point. The first, the parable of the straying
sheep, as we have seen, stresses the importance of making
every effort to bring back into the community those who have
strayed. The second, the unjust steward in 18.23-35, makes a
rather different point. Just as the highest virtue is forgiveness, so too those who have experienced forgiveness and
refuse themselves to forgive have the greatest fault. In such
circumstances, we are told, they deserve to be excluded: 'the
lord delivered him to the jailers until he should pay all his
debt' (18.34).

Matthew's Sectarianism

What can one say about the type of community which
Matthew was helping to build? Both Luz (*Matthew 1–7*,
p. 219) and Overman (*Matthew's Gospel*, p. 154) have suggested that it is helpful to characterize Matthew's community as a sect. This is, of course, a very elastic term and
might seem to some to suggest a group which is simply
obscurantist. It certainly suggests a sense of opposition to
the prevailing forces in society. As a term it was used by
Ernst Troeltsch in contradistinction to 'church'. A church, as
an institution which dispenses salvation, is marked by a religion of grace and a piety of redemption. A sect, by contrast,
as a free association of strict and conscious Christians has a
religion of law and makes more vigorous efforts to establish a
Christian way of life based on love. In such a group Christ is
lord, example and lawgiver, rather than first and foremost a
redeemer figure. Achieving holiness is what is of primary
importance for the group; redemption is expected in the
future.

Luz acknowledges his debt to Troeltsch and his conviction
that in these terms Matthew's *theology* offers a classic
example of sectarian theology. It is the theology of a
minority group which takes Jesus as its leader in its quest to
establish its own way of life based on obedience and love. It is

perfectionist, a religion centred on law, where grace is essentially practical assistance. As we shall very shortly see, in the course of church history Matthew's Gospel has often provided marginalized groups with theological support, just as it has been such groups who have attempted to live out its demands most strictly.

Overman draws his definition of sect from the British sociologist Bryan Wilson. Here sects are defined in terms of their 'response to the world', that is, to the dominant groupings within their environment who determine the social and cultural norms. Characteristically sects develop strategies for enforcing their own norms against those of the wider society by setting tight boundaries around their group, by polemic against the dominant group and its leaders, and by consolidating and legitimizing their own structures and norms. Much of Overman's book is given over to showing patterns of sectarian behaviour within Judaism of the first century. These patterns of behaviour have he believes had a considerable influence on Matthew's community which was 'clearly sectarian' (p. 154). It was a minority over against the parent group, formative Judaism out of which Rabbinic Judaism emerged. The harsh language of the Gospel against the Jewish leadership betrays its sense of marginalization. It was, relatively speaking, 'more concerned with world-maintenance than being open to the world...interested in community formation, and not primarily world transformation' (p. 154).

The term 'sectarian', as used by Wilson, covers a variety of social groups, all of which are more or less sharply distinguished from the dominant society within which they live. Among the different types of sects, however, it is important to distinguish different responses to the world outside. It is one of the weaknesses of both Luz's and Overman's analyses that they do not address this question sufficiently clearly. Luz is more concerned to identify certain typical theological features of the sect; while Overman assumes too easily that the identification of certain features—polemics against the leaders of the majority society, the search for legitimation, community building—speaks for a particular type of sect, namely one that is interesting in maintaining its own life rather than in transforming the wider society. This is strange in view of the missionary emphasis of the conclusion of the Gospel. There is of course, as we have seen, clear evidence that Matthew was interested in providing norms for his community, in dealing with matters of community discipline and with sharply distinguishing his church from the synagogue. One might add that there is also a shift in the way in which motifs concerning the end of the world are employed. If for Mark the foretelling of an end to the world as it is presently known (ch. 13) is a way of underscoring the need to part company with the ways of this world, in Matthew the depiction of the last judgment in the parable of the sheep and the goats in ch. 25 is designed to reinforce the norms of the new community. So there is undoubtedly a sense in which Matthew's community is setting itself up as an alternative society with its own norms contrasted with those of its Jewish neighbour, while still claiming common roots in the Torah. But this does not mean to say that it is not interested in world-transformation: it claims authority over the whole world for the Son and sends its members out into the world to make disciples of all. It may have turned its back on Judaism but this was only to take up the task of the Jewish nation to proclaim God's rule in all the world and to bring all the peoples to acknowledge it.

The Gospel in Later Communities

We have been considering Matthew's contribution to the formation of the early church communities for whom he wrote. Of course we can only speculate about the actual effect which the Gospel may have had on those communities. To be quite clear, we cannot make more than informed guesses about their actual situation. It is, however, interesting to ask what the continuing role of the Gospel was in the development of the church. How was it read by later communities and how did it contribute to the particular form which those communities took?

This takes us into the realm of what is sometimes called 'history of effects'. This is a somewhat awkward translation of the German *Wirkungsgeschichte*. It is a study of the way in which certain texts have a history in terms of the literary traditions, social communities, attitudes, political consequences which they engender. It is usually distinguished from the history of interpretation in that it is not just concerned with cataloguing the different ways in which commentators have read the texts, but is also interested in the wider implications and impact which texts have had in the course of time. For Matthew we are particularly well served by Luz's commentary which has made study of the history of effects into a valuable tool for understanding the 'potential for meaning' (*Sinnpotential*) of texts. His claim is that we fully understand the meaning of texts only when we have seen their potential for generating a wider set of meanings which can be embodied in different communities.

We can here give only a sample of what this approach contributes to the understanding of Matthew's Gospel and will do so in relation to the beatitudes and the antitheses of the Sermon on the Mount. These are clearly central texts and ones which Luz has discussed not only in his commentary but in other places as well.

The Beatitudes
We first need to situate Matthew's own redaction of the beatitudes within a continuum of development from Jesus. According to Luz (*Matthew 1–7*, pp. 227-29), whose views I am summarizing throughout this section, it is likely that three beatitudes go back to Jesus: those addressed to the poor, the hungry and those that weep. Here Jesus is proclaiming the unrestricted grace of God to the disadvantaged, regardless of anything that they may have done to earn it. And the blessings that he announces are already to be experienced in the dawning of the Kingdom in Jesus' activity, 'in his turning to the poor, in the love which he lived and called for' (*Nachfolge und Bergpredigt*, p. 40).

Other beatitudes were added in the course of time. Q probably added a fourth to Jesus' original three: 5.11-12 which announces blessing to those in the congregation who are persecuted. That is to say the blessings are being interpreted as addressed to the congregation and not simply to the disadvantaged in the world. A further four were added

before Matthew came to write: vv.5, 7-9, all of which are
addressed to those who possess certain ethical characteristics, among which are those which tend towards a certain
'inwardness': humility, purity of heart. Finally Matthew
added v. 10: 'Blessed are those who are persecuted for righteousness' sake, for theirs is the kingdom of heaven' and
added the reference to righteousness in v. 6. The effect of this
is again to emphasize the particular concrete action which
denotes the blessed, rather than simply to point to the situation in which they happen to find themselves.

That is to say, there is a major change in the use of the
beatitudes between Jesus and Matthew. Whereas Jesus
preached salvation to the poor and suffering, Matthew holds
up a 'mirror of virtues' to his congregation. So striking is this
reworking of the tradition that we have to question its legitimacy. Luz wants to affirm it. The situation of those who first
heard Jesus' proclamation of radical grace is altogether
different from that of Matthew's hearers who had grown too
accustomed to it and now needed to be reminded of its
demands. 'The problem of Matthew's congregations seems to
be how properly to remain within grace' (*Nachfolge und
Bergpredigt*, p. 42). Matthew uses his creative fantasy to
address such problems. He does not merely change the mode
of the beatitudes from indicative to imperative; he embeds
the demands of the beatitudes in the story of God's gracious
dealings with his people in his Son Jesus.

The history of the appropriation of this text by later
generations is one which divides into three. Some interpreters stress the imparting of grace to those who are
unworthy. In the classical interpretation of the early church
the ethical aspects of the texts are stressed. For Gregory of
Nyssa the beatitudes constitute a royal stairway which leads
from the first movement of repentance to the Christian's final
perfection. The individual beatitudes are interpreted
ethically, so that 'poor in spirit' is taken to refer to the
humble. (*Matthew 1-7*, p. 234) Alongside this, in certain
monastic and clerical traditions, where the way of the perfect
is distinguished from that of the normal Christians, it is
taken to refer to voluntary (taking 'in spirit' to mean 'by decision of the human spirit') material poverty. This tradition of

ethical interpretation which contrasts with Jesus' announcing the radical grace of God continues down to the first Reformers. Luther speaks of the commandments which the Gospel contains (p. 234).

However, in the second generation of the Reformation a more Pauline interpretation begins to be developed. 'Poor in spirit' is understood as 'being conscious of sin' and taken to refer to those who 'seized by the experience of their sins, far from all pride, subject themselves to God' (Theodore of Beza). Similarly 'thirsting for justice' is understood as longing for the divine grace of imputed righteousness (A. Calov) and Bengel stresses that it precisely does not say 'blessed are the righteous'. Thus read from a different (Pauline) perspective the texts are largely purged of their strong ethical note (*Nachfolge und Bergpredigt*, p. 44; cf. *Matthew 1–7*, p. 237). While this clearly overlooks significant elements in the text, such interpretations do bring out the tendency towards inwardness which we noticed in Matthew's tradition.

At the risk of great simplification we may say that the early church interpretations with their strong emphasis on the ethical demands of the Gospel provide the basis for an embodiment of Christian norms in a Christian community, whether this was conceived as an alternative to the dominant society, as with Matthew and as in the first three centuries, or whether it was conceived as coterminous with society as a whole, as in the period of imperial recognition of Christianity. By contrast, the Protestant interpretations, notably those from a Lutheran tradition, show the way in which Christianity can develop into a religion of inwardness which then allows the state gradually to assume control of the moral regulation of society. On the other hand it has to be said that the later Protestant readings are faithful to one aspect of Matthew's handling of the beatitudes, namely his tendency to interiorize them.

The Antitheses
As Luz shows, such tendencies become even more striking when we come to look at the antitheses, the sayings which employ some such formula as 'you have heard that it was said to those of old...but I say to you'. Again there has been

development in the tradition between Jesus and Matthew. Jesus probably only uttered two sayings in this form: those about murder and adultery (*Matthew 1–7*, pp. 274-76). Moreover he probably understood the passive 'it was said' as a divine passive (an indirect way of referring to God, i.e. with the meaning 'God said') and 'those of old' to refer to the generation of Sinai. Thus Jesus is contrasting his authority with the authority of the divine revelation on Sinai. This an amazing contrast, particularly in light of the fact that what he actually asserts is in many ways no more than 'rabbinic commonsense'. Nevertheless, Jesus is not interested in legislation, in working out the practical details of the interpretation and application of the Law. His sayings offer exhortation, often with an element of the impractical. What would it be for a Galilean to leave his gift and go back home to settle a dispute while on his way to Jerusalem? Such extravagance has its location within Jesus' expectation of a dramatic inbreaking of the Kingdom of God (*Nachfolge und Bergpredigt*, p. 51).

Matthew's treatment of the antitheses is characterized by two striking features: (1) that he chooses as the first and the last antitheses sayings which deal with love and hatred (cf. too the summary of the Law in 7.12); thus there is a strong suggestion that it is the love command which provides the key to all Jesus' sayings about the Law and indeed to the understanding of the Law in general; (2) that he prefaces the whole sermon with the strongest possible affirmation of the continuing significance of the Law; thus sayings of Jesus which originally contrasted the authority of the Law with his own now become sayings which at most intensify the meaning of the Law. This creates a tension where there is serious conflict between Jesus' sayings and the Law, as with the sayings about non-retaliation.

The history of effects shows quite clearly how these tensions can generate very different readings of the Matthaean antitheses (see as well as the detailed discussions in Luz's commentary, and in *Nachfolge und Bergpredigt*, pp. 53-62). Luz focuses attention particularly on the differences at the time of the Reformation between mainline Reformers and the Anabaptists. The Anabaptists, who

quickly became the subject of brutal repression, took and
applied the antitheses literally. They saw them as contrasted
with the Old Testament Law and therefore understood the
New Testament as the proclamation of a new and better law.
(Unlike Matthew they had no need to show the continuity
between their ethic and the Law, for the Jews were by now in
a very different position of influence.) This in turn led them
to apply the commands of the Sermon on the Mount very
seriously. Thus they refused to take oaths or to carry arms.
In part, this may have been the result of a rather biblicist
approach; in part, the outcome of a lay approach to theology,
which did not have sophisticated theological schemata at its
disposal to enable them to finesse the sharper demands of
the Sermon. More importantly there is a recognition here of
the character of the Gospel as Law. The Swiss Anabaptist,
Hans Denck wrote:

> Whoever finds.God's command difficult, does not love God and
> does not know him, how good he is...God's covenant and the yoke
> of his Son is heavy only to those who have not carried it...The
> more the elect works in God's vineyard, the less he tires; even the
> work is rest for him in God' (quoted in *Nachfolge und Bergpredigt*,
> p. 55).

By contrast, the mainline Reformers saw the antitheses as
correctives to Jewish misinterpretation of the Law.
Particularly for Calvin, there could be nothing wrong with
the Law that Jesus would have needed to modify. This in
turn led him to play down the force of Jesus' commands in
the antitheses, not least his injunction to shun the use of
violence.

Further, the Reformers tended to read Jesus' commandments in the light of the love command and thus to soften
their demands. Christians were enjoined to consider the
effects of their actions on their dependents. In general this
led to an ethic of motive (it's the intention which counts),
whereas the Anabaptists argued that the commandments
gave concrete expression to the love command.

What is noticeable too is the lack of real conviction on the
part of the Reformers that Jesus' commandments could be
lived out either by individuals or by the church as a whole.
People were permanently sinful, *simul justus et peccator*, and

therefore the best one could do was to preach repentance and
grace to the individual. By contrast the Anabaptists sought
to create a holy community, faithful to Jesus' teaching.

As Luz points out there is much in common between the
Anabaptists and Matthew. In their emphasis on the gracious
character of Jesus' commandments, in their understanding of
discipleship as the keeping of the commandments, as a way
of righteousness which Christ helps the believers to follow so
that they may enter life (Mt. 7.13), in their attempts to forge
a community which would live out the life of discipleship,
they were close to Matthew's intentions and to the situation
of his communities. Like him, they were a closed, somewhat
sectarian group, at odds with the world around them but
trying to live out their ideals with some intensity in the
fellowship of the group. The Reformers, by contrast, were
attempting to create a new society in which the church would
be an important institution. They were much more cautious
about the application of the radical ethic of the Gospel to
their societies, which had to defend themselves and admin-
ister a legal system with binding oaths. For this reason, they
gladly seized upon those elements in Matthew which could
allow them to soften the demands of Jesus' kingdom ethic
and which would make it more serviceable as a civil code.
They would also enthusiastically develop the tendencies
already present in Matthew, and indeed in his tradition,
towards an interiorization of the Gospel.

The story of the appropriation of the Sermon on the Mount
in Christian history brings out very clearly the contrary tendencies within the text itself. As Luz shows, these are themselves the result of a complex history in which the early
Christian community has attempted to live out Jesus' teaching and preaching. As circumstances changed, and indeed as
theological emphases shifted, so the tradition developed and
was moulded until it was written down in the form of
Matthew's Gospel. Subsequent generations, from their own
standpoints, have also contributed to the development of this
tradition by the way they have emphasized different aspects
of the text and indeed by the way that they have interpreted
and given imaginative life to them. Those who wish to
engage creatively in this continuing process of appropriation

of Matthew's Gospel will do well to be aware both of the diversity of interpretations there have been and also of the way in which such interpretations are rooted in the text. This will both encourage fresh and open readings of these texts, as readers bring their own perspectives to bear on them, and also close readings, as they allow their readings to be challenged and informed by the complex meanings of Matthew's composition.

Further Reading

J. Barclay, *Obeying the Truth* (Edinburgh: T. & T. Clark, 1988).

G. Bornkamm, 'Der Aufbau der Bergpredigt', *NTS* 24 (1977–78), pp. 419-32.

P. Berger, *The Sacred Canopy: Elements of a Sociological Theory of Religion* (Garden City, NY: Doubleday, 1969).

W.D. Davies, *The Setting of the Sermon on the Mount* (Cambridge: Cambridge University Press, 1966).

M. Hengel, 'Between Jesus and Paul', in *Between Jesus and Paul* (London: SCM Press, 1983), pp. 1-29.

U. Luz, 'Die Bergpredigt im Spiegel ihrer Wirkungsgeschichte', in J. Moltmann (ed.), *Nachfolge und Bergpredigt* (Munich: Chr. Kaiser Verlag, 1981).

J.L. Martyn, *History and Theology in the Fourth Gospel* (New York: Harper and Row, 1968).

J.A. Overmann, *Matthew's Gospel and Formative Judaism* (Minneapolis: Fortress Press, 1990).

E.P. Sanders, *Judaism: Practice and Belief* (London: SCM Press, 1992).

K. Stendahl, *The School of Matthew and its Use of the Old Testament* (Philadelphia: Fortress Press, 2nd edn, 1968).

G. Theissen, *The First Followers of Jesus* (London: SCM Press, 1978).

W. Trilling, *Das wahre Israel: Studien zur Theologie des Matthäusevangeliums* (Munich: Kosel, 1964).

4

MATTHEW'S CHRISTOLOGY

SO FAR WE HAVE BEEN looking at the kind of book that
Matthew's Gospel is, at the ways in which it was written and
at the broader context in the life of the church and of
Judaism in which it was set. But what was Matthew trying
to say to his readers? What specifically did he want to say
about Jesus and about God? It is reasonable to suppose that
a first-century writer close to the Jewish tradition who writes
a book in which the central figure is acclaimed by God at his
baptism and transfiguration as his son is making theological
claims.

But how are we to get at the central theological import of
the Gospel? Part of the problem is connected with the way in
which New Testament scholars have approached theological
questions; part is related to divergences of approach to
Matthew's Gospel. Let me explain.

1. When scholars first started to look at the New
Testament historically and critically in the eighteenth
century, the more radical spirits, like H.S. Reimarus, questioned how far the New Testament could support the views of
Jesus' divinity that were set out in the creeds. It could be
fairly convincingly shown that the title 'son of God', for
instance, in its Old Testament usage did not mean anything
like 'the second person of the Trinity'. A fully fledged doctrine
of the Trinity is indeed a product of some centuries of
Christian reflection. The question is then how far such developments are already prefigured in the New Testament
writings themselves. When biblical terms like 'son of God'
were used by the New Testament writers were they being

filled with new meaning? What other terms were employed to express early Christian beliefs about Jesus' theological status? What other means were used to express nascent Christian beliefs in Jesus' divinity? Did Jesus himself claim some kind of special relationship to God? Did such beliefs originate in early Christianity itself and, if so, at what point?

Such questions are clearly of major importance to Christian theologians and of considerable interest to others too. It is not however our task to tell the story of their scholarly investigation. Two points are pertinent here. First, perhaps rather unsurprisingly, much of the debate has been conducted in terms of christological titles. This is obviously important as such titles represent an important part of first-century linguistic resources for making theological statements. But there are other linguistic resources. Imagery and metaphor, such as that deployed in the Fourth Gospel, typology and scriptural allusion, may also tell us much about the Evangelists' views of Jesus' theological status. The way the Evangelists narrated Jesus' story, the range of literary techniques which they employed, may tell us a great deal about who they thought he was.

The second point is related. Until some 30 years ago scholars had tended to focus attention either on the theological titles in the epistles and the long discourses of the Fourth Gospel or on the development of such titles in the tradition which lay behind the Synoptic Gospels. They had paid little attention to the way in which the Synoptic Evangelists set out their views about Jesus' status. The most notable exception to this was William Wrede's discussion of the Messianic secret. Jesus' commands to silence, his parable theory, and the disciples' lack of understanding were identified by Wrede as motifs in the Gospels which were making a theological point about Jesus. He was, however, less certain about whether such motifs were to be attributed to the early Christian communities or to the Evangelists, above all Mark, themselves. With the rise of redaction criticism in the late 50s attention at last turned to the Evangelists. Even so, initially, it was the titles which formed the centre of discussion. Interest in the Evangelist's 'narrative christology' is a relatively recent phenomenon.

2. The other part of the problem is related to the approach taken to the Gospels. Do we see the Gospels as the outcome of a complex literary process of production, which process can give us the clue to the intended senses of their editors? Or do we see them as literary works in themselves, which can yield up their secrets to an eye trained to recognize the complex relationships between the various parts, motifs, plots, characters, authorial devices etc. which go to make up the whole? The former view will take very seriously the literary *history* of which Matthew's Gospel is a part; the latter will treat it as an isolated phenomenon which can stand on its own. It is fashionable to characterize such views as on the one hand historical, on the other literary-critical. This seems to me to be dangerously misleading: both are interested in literary texts which are part of the culture of a particular age; the question at issue is whether one believes that the appreciation of such texts is assisted or hindered by attending to the historical circumstances of their production and reception. Interestingly, as we shall see, more attention to the narrative or literary character of Matthew's christology is paid by those who would often be characterized as working in a purely historical critical mode.

Kingsbury's Account of Matthaean Christology

Kingsbury, whom we have already met in conjunction with literary discusions of the Gospel, has raised questions about Matthew's christology which have prompted vigorous debate. In his first major contribution to this area, *Matthew: Structure, Christology, Kingdom*, Kingsbury argued that 'Son of God' is the 'central christological category of Matthew's Gospel' (p. 82) and that it is in the light of this title that all the others are to be interpreted. 'Son of God' is the one title that is found distributed across all the major parts of the Gospel; it is found at the major events of Jesus' baptism (3.17), temptation (4.3, 6), after the walking on the water (14.33), at Peter's confession at Caesarea Philippi (16.16), at the transfiguration (17.5), at the trial (26.63) and crucifixion (27.40, 54). But this is not all. Kingsbury believes that the title lies behind much of the other material in the Gospel (the

references to the Son and Jesus' address to God as 'my
Father'—many Matthew's own) and that it is presupposed in
the account of the resurrection. Thus, for instance, when
Jesus goes up on to the mountain at 5.1 to deliver the
Sermon on the Mount, this is an indirect allusion to his
Sonship. This might be surprising, but Kingsbury asserts
that 'the mountain is the place of eschatological revelation'
(pp. 56-57), listing 4.8; 5.1; 15.29; 17.1; 28.16 (of which he
notes all but 17.1 as Matthew's own addition or creation). He
sees the reference to Emmanuel ('God with us') in 1.23 and
echoed in 18.20 and 28.20 (and, he argues, 14.27) as
containing *in nuce* everything that Matthew otherwise says
in 1.1–4.16 of Jesus Son of God' (p. 53). The title is distinguished by being a 'confessional' one (hence its relative
scarcity in the long section on Jesus' public ministry,
4.17–10.42—the demon in 8.29 knows who Jesus is even if he
does not confess him); where it is used by non-believers, it is
blasphemous. It is revealed to those who make the confession. This distinguishes it from one of the other major titles
in the Gospel, Son of Man, which Kingsbury sees as a public
title, addressed only to those outside the group of disciples. It
does not occur until 8.20 and 'except for the "righteous" in
the scene of the Last Judgment, it marks the people in view
of whom it is used as being unbelievers or opponents of
Jesus' (p. 115). Its principal interest for Matthew is in its
reference to Jesus as the eschatological judge; in this respect
it 'coalesces' with the title Son of God (p. 121).

Later in *Matthew as Story* Kingsbury argued the same
case on rather different grounds. If in his first book he was
working as a redaction critic, looking to see what changes
Matthew had made in his sources, attending to patterns of
usage and emphasis throughout the book, here he dons the
robe of the *ahistorical* literary critic. Historical considera-
tions of setting, sources, mode of composition are set aside
and we are invited to attend to the composition itself and to
the literary conventions by which writers can make themselves heard. Two points are crucial to Kingsbury's argument
in this book. First, he now pays greater attention to the
placing of the titles within the Gospel itself. Son of God is
seen to occur as the culmination of each of the three major

sections which Kingsbury has identified: 1.1–4.16; 4.17–16.20; 16.21–end. Secondly, he distinguishes the various 'points of view' which are presented in the Gospel. In simple terms we need to distinguish between the point of view of the author, of Jesus and of God. It is clear that in the Gospel Jesus' point of view and that of the author coincide. What is interesting is that these receive ultimate accreditation from the entry of God as 'actor' in the divine voice in 3.17 and 17.5 where God declares Jesus to be his beloved son. Thus the ultimately authoritative point of view in the Gospel accredits the title 'Son of God' as the one truly authoritative title in the light of which all others have to be read.

There is a further aspect to this literary approach to the question of Matthew's christology which concerns his use of the Son of Man title. Kingsbury has argued that it is 'Son of God' as opposed to 'Son of Man' which represents God's point of view in the Gospel and this is reinforced for him by the fact that in the first section 1.1–4.16 which sets out who Jesus is, the title 'Son of Man' does not occur. Furthermore, he argues, its use in Matthew is quite distinct from that of other titles, which are used to say 'who Jesus is', whereas the phrase 'Son of Man' occurs only on Jesus' lips and is never used predicatively (i.e. in the form 'I am the Son of Man'). ' "The Son of Man" is not meant to clarify for the reader who Jesus is but must itself be clarified' ('Figure', p. 23).

Rather strangely, he finds confirmation of this view in his discussion of the trial scene before the High Priest. Jesus' reply to the High Priest's demand: 'tell us if you are the Christ, the Son of God' is 'You have said so'. Kingsbury takes this as a straight affirmative and reads Jesus' subsequent remark 'But I tell you hereafter you will see the Son of Man seated at the right hand of power...' as merely a 'tacit reference to himself as "the Son of Man" ' ('Figure', p. 23). The reason for this is twofold: one that he rightly observes that the title is nowhere picked up by those to whom it is uttered. In this case the priests in mocking him refer to him as Christ. The other is that he wants to translate the phrase not as a special title, carrying certain sense contents, but as a mode of self-reference, 'this man'.

What then is the purpose, according to Kingsbury, of

Matthew's use of the phrase? ' "The Son of Man" may be
defined as the title by means of which Jesus refers to himself
"in public" or in view of the "public" (or "world")...as "the
man", or "the human being" (earthly, suffering, vindicated),
and to assert his divine authority in the face of opposition'
('Figure', p. 27). By speaking of 'Son of Man' as a public title,
Kingsbury means two things: first, that it is principally
addressed to the world; secondly, that it can be used openly
without any of those who are addressed actually picking it up
and using it. How is it to be understood? The key is in the
exchange between Jesus and Peter at Caesarea Philippi:
Jesus (not Peter, as Kingsbury rather oddly suggests) asks
who is the Son of Man and Peter replies, You are the Son of
God.

It might seem then that Kingsbury is saying that the term
has no content at all. Nevertheless, he does suggest that it is
'associated' with Jesus' assertion of his divine authority
('Figure', p. 29) and that it is a phrase used specifically in situations of opposition. It signifies the opposition which Jesus
encounters as well as pointing to his ultimate vindication,
themes which Kingsbury shows, without too much difficulty,
run through the Gospel.

Thus Kingsbury's literary critical analysis neatly confirms
his earlier findings about Matthew's christology. While there
has been general agreement among scholars that Kingsbury
has been right to highlight the importance of Son of God in
Matthew's Gospel, there is much less agreement that it
should be seen as the central title. One of Kingsbury's most
persistent critics, David Hill, has suggested that overvaluing
the Son of God title leads to a lack of sensitivity to the many
other rich allusions which are to be found in the text. Hill
himself has drawn attention to the importance for Matthew
of the Servant of Yahweh imagery of Isaiah which is
presented in the long quotation of Isa. 42.1-4 in Mt. 12.18-21,
alluded to by the divine voice in 3.17 and 17.5 and the citation of Isaiah 53 at 8.17. Hill's point is not that the image of
Servant is more important than the title Son of God, but
rather that the image gives *content* to the title which otherwise in Kingsbury's treatment seems only to refer to Jesus'
authority, whereas the Servant image would associate it with

notions of healing and atonement. Hill's own work shows the
value of exploring the intertextual relationships between
Matthew and the Old Testament. He suggests that the
quotation of Isaiah 42 at 12.18-21 is substantially modified
by Matthew himself in the light of the divine voice in 3.17, at
the same time as the quotation itself shapes chapter 12,
emphasizing Jesus' empowerment by the Spirit and his
humility and his saving concern for 'the weak, the lost and
the broken' ('Son and Servant', p. 12).

Hill is equally critical of Kingsbury's treatment of Son of
Man in Matthew. Of *Matthew: Structure, Christology,
Kingship* Hill says that its treatment of the evidence is
'Procrustean' ('Son and Servant', p. 2), forcing it to conform
to his own preconceived ideas. Why should the scribe in 8.18-
20 be regarded as in opposition to Jesus? Again, is it credible
that 'Matthew can use "Son of Man" at 20.28 only because it
is the mother of James and John (i.e. an unbeliever or
opponent?) whose request provokes the utterance?' ('Son and
Servant', p. 3). And he rightly turns to Kingsbury's treatment of the trial before the High Priest to ask why there is
no discussion there (or anywhere else) of Daniel 7 to which
there is clear allusion in Jesus' reply.

Similar suggestions have been made by Dale Allison, the
co-author with W.D. Davies of the new ICC commentary on
Matthew. In an early article ('Son of God as Israel', pp. 74-
81), Allison suggests that Kingsbury's concentration on the
text alone, irrespective of its roots in and allusions to the Old
Testament denies to him insights which would have enriched
his work. Not only are there clear allusions to the Servant of
Yahweh from Isaiah, as Hill has pointed out, there is also a
strong typological interplay between the notion of Jesus as
Son of God and that of Israel as God's Son (something that
R.E. Brown has also argued in *The Birth of the Messiah*).
This is seen most clearly in the quotation of Hos. 11.1 at
2.15: 'Out of Egypt have I called my son', which in Hosea
clearly refers to Israel and in Matthew points to the close
parallels between Jesus' story and Israel's. Thus when Jesus
is addressed by the divine voice in 3.17 as 'my beloved Son' is
he not 'also here identified in some sense with Israel?' (p. 76;
note that the page numbers need renumbering: read in the

following order: 74, 75, 78, 79, 76, 77, 80, 81). Israel's history of exodus, wanderings in the desert and revelation on the mountain is mirrored in Jesus' story in Matthew.

Allison on Jesus as the New Moses

Recently Allison has developed this kind of approach in an excellent study of Moses typology in ancient literature and in Matthew, *The New Moses*. The value of this book is that it both sets out clear criteria for identifying typological allusions, and that it provides a full survey of the use of Moses as a typological figure in a wide range of ancient texts prior to Matthew's Gospel. This certainly helps to give an element of precision and control to this kind of discussion, which is needed.

Allison identifies six kinds of textual allusion to figures or events from the past:

1. Explicit statement: Jn 3.14 refers directly to the incident with Moses and the serpent.
2. Inexplicit citation or borrowing: Mk 1.6 in referring to John's leather girdle actually cites words from the Greek translation of 2 Kgs 1.8 about Elijah.
3. Similar circumstances: Joshua's crossing of the Jordan may be intended to recall Moses' crossing of the Red Sea.
4. Key words or phrases: the Gospel accounts of the miraculous feedings pick up the barley loaves which are mentioned in the miraculous feeding in 2 Kgs 4.42-44.
5. Similar narrative structure: Mark's account of the calling of the disciples in 1.16-20 is structurally close to that in 1 Kgs 19.19-21.
6. Word order, syllabic sequence, poetic resonance. In Jn 1.1 there are clear echoes of Gen. 1.1, not only in its identical 'in the beginning' but also in the rhythmic and syllabic structure in the Greek (pp. 19-21).

Given this variety, we need some guide as to where we can be confident of intended allusions. Allison lays down three conditions, which if satisfied make it likely that the author intended an allusion:

1.   Priority in time: the work alluded to must precede
      that in which the allusion is made and intended.
2.   The tradition or book referred to must have been
      known to the author making the allusion.
3.   Unless there is explicit allusion, a *combination* of
      features 3-6 above is required if we are to be confident
      that there has been an intentional allusion on the
      part of the author.
4.   The type referred to should be prominent.
5.   The alleged typology is more likely if frequently used.
6.   The more unusual the shared imagery, motifs, etc.
      the more likely there is an intended connection
      (pp. 21-23).

The strength of Allison's argument depends very much on
his careful demonstration of the richness of typological allusion that is to be found in Jewish literature prior to
Matthew. He demonstrates, that is to say, that this was a
widespread cultural phenomenon which was employed to
link key figures in Israel's history, Moses with Joshua,
Gideon, David, Jeremiah, the promised Messiah, to show the
continuity of God's dealings with his people. In this Moses
may function as type in various capacities: as leader/king
(Joshua, Josiah), as saviour/deliverer (Gideon, Messiah), as
lawgiver/teacher (Ezra, Ezekiel, Hillel), and as intercessor/
suffering prophet (Jeremiah and the Servant in Deutero-
Isaiah). What is noteworthy is that in most cases the connection is *not* made explicit and that therefore the readers are
required to pick up the allusions for themselves. Such
comparisons (and comparison/*sugkrasis* was a widespread
phenomenon in the ancient world) clearly served to exalt the
figure who was being compared to, for example, Moses. They
were not, however, by any means the only points which were
being made; rather they occur alongside any number of
differences in the accounts. Finally, Allison notes that all the
extensive literature covered in his survey was known to
Matthew (*New Moses*, part I).

How then does Matthew himself deploy such Moses typology in relation to Jesus? There is not room to discuss
Allison's treatment of the whole Gospel but only to look at
one section: the infancy narratives (pp. 140-65). Allison finds

evidence of textual linking under all the heads mentioned above except the last. The treatment is full but a selection of the points may indicate its persuasiveness.

1. Explicit citation of the Exodus story occurs in 2.15 where Matthew cites Hos. 11.1. Noting that this is in the first place a reference to Israel rather than Moses, Allison avers that they are correlative conceptions.

2. Inexplicit citation: Allison notes a number of close similarities in the accounts of Mt. 2.19-21 and Exod. 4.19-20, some of which look like verbal echoes of the Exodus account. Both Moses and Jesus go into exile until the king who is pursuing them dies (Matthew's account 'those seeking the life of the child have died' echoes closely that of Exodus 'all those seeking your life have died'). This intelligence is communicated supernaturally and the two protagonists return with their family.

3. Similar circumstances: comparing Matthew's narra-tive with the Moses story in later Jewish tradition (Josephus and the targums—Aramaic translations of the Hebrew Bible) Allison notes that in both the fathers are worried about the mother's pregnancy (see Josephus, *Ant.* 2.210-16); both figures are known as saviours (2.228); in both cases the order is given for the slaughter of all the male children because the king learns of the birth of a future liberator of the people (2.205-209), from scribes (2.205, 234) and magi (Jerusalem targum on Exod. 1.15); both kings are disturbed when they hear the prophecy (*Ant.* 2.206).

4. Key-words and phrases: see above under 3.

5. Similar narrative structure: Allison believes that he can discern a similar tri-partite structure containing two dreams experienced by the father and the persecutor and then the birth and deliverance of the saviour.

While individual details of this might be disputed, and while there is obviously a problem about the reliance on Josephus who is at best a contemporary of Matthew, the evidence accumulated here and in Allison's continuing discussion of the rest of the Gospel is undeniably impressive. At the end of his treatment, Allison summarizes his findings as follows (*New Moses*, pp. 267-70).

The Moses typology is one theme among many, a main branch rather than the trunk itself. It is especially strong in the Infancy narratives and the Sermon on the Mount and generally shapes chs. 1–7 with the infancy, crossing of the water at baptism, temptation in the wilderness, and law-giving. Subsequently there are important further allusions in the sayings about the reciprocal knowledge of Father and Son, in the transfiguration where Moses himself appears and in the commissioning of Jesus' successors in 28.16-20. In all this Matthew is following established conventions of typology. The typology is moreover for the most part hidden: Moses is named only seven times.

What implications does this have for our understanding of Matthew's christology? Fundamentally, Matthew, by developing the comparison between Jesus and Moses, is attempting to root the new dispensation in the old, 'to pour new wine into old wineskins'. Matthew draws freely on the typological resources of the tradition: Jesus, by dint of the comparison with Moses, is seen as the prophet-king, as the Messiah, the miracle worker, the giver of Torah, the mediator for Israel and the suffering servant. What is interesting in all this is that there is no polemic against Moses. Moses is the typological herald and foreshadower of Jesus as the law-giver, not his rival. However, in developing such a broad comparison, one theme is of particular importance: that of Jesus' *exousia*, authority (cf. 7.29; 8.27; 9.6; 10.1; 21.27; 28.18). Just as Moses is the incorporation of authority for the Jews, so too is Jesus for the church. The Sermon on the Mount culminates in the crowd's exclamation that Jesus teaches as having authority; 11.25-30 declares that all things have been revealed to Jesus; at the transfiguration the voice from heaven declares that they are to 'listen to him'; and in the final commissioning Jesus declares that all authority has been given to him. According to Allison, Matthew 'draped the Messiah in the familiar mantle of Moses, by which dress he made Jesus the full bearer of God's authority' (p. 277).

It will be clear that I regard this as an important and

instructive book. The question of Jesus' relation to Moses
is of course not new. It was raised, as we have, seen by
B.S. Bacon with his suggestion of a fivefold structure to the
Gospel, mirroring the five books of the Law. Others,
including W.D. Davies and R.E. Brown, have explored the
use of this kind of typology in Matthew's Gospel. The merits
of Allison's treatment lie in his careful portrayal of the ways
in which ancient Hebrew texts develop the Moses typology
and then in his use of this knowledge to track down
Matthew's intention through the Gospel. The question which
it raises most acutely, precisely because of its careful and
thorough documentation of the Moses typology in Jewish
(and Christian) tradition, concerns the extent to which Jesus
is seen, as is Joshua, as like but essentially subordinate to
Moses; to what extent he is seen as replacing Moses as a
figure of authority in Judaism. Allison is very keen to stress
the continuity which is implied in such typological treatment. According to him, the purpose of such a comparison is
precisely to remind the church of its roots in Judaism as it is
casting or being cast loose from its parent body. Yet on any
reading it should be clear that what is occurring is in many
respects different from what occurs in Jewish tradition.

Clearly there are intended similarities. Jesus, like Moses,
instructs the people, imparts to them the will of God. What
he teaches is consistent with, 'fulfils', the Law and the
prophets (5.17; 7.12). In 23.2-3, the crowds and the disciples
are told to obey the scribes and Pharisees because 'they sit on
Moses' seat.' These are texts which are only found as such in
Matthew. There are others which Matthew has taken over
from Mark which also stress the continuity. Jesus commands
the leper to show himself to the priest and to offer the gift as
Moses commanded (Mt. 8.4). In 17.3-4 he is transfigured with
Moses and Elijah (here Matthew has changed Mark's 'Elijah
with Moses' to 'Moses and Elijah'—orders of precedence were
important in the ancient world). But while Matthew thus
asserts that what Jesus does is consistent with the work of
Moses, that is to say that God is acting through him in a
manner which is in accord with the way he acted through
Moses, there are distinctions to be made. What Jesus teaches
is contrasted with Moses' teaching. In the antitheses in the

Sermon on the Mount (a feature Matthew has developed, contrast Luke's three occurrences with Matthew's six) Jesus contrasts his teaching with what they have heard of old. In the controversy over divorce, Jesus' indicates that Moses' teaching is given for the hardness of their hearts and is to be replaced by his own re-emphasis of the creator's purposes in creating male and female. Again, in the transfiguration, while Jesus is associated with Moses and Elijah, he is also singled out by the divine voice as the beloved Son, as the one to whom the disciples must listen (17.5). Similarly, but with greater clarity and emphasis, Jesus at the end of the Gospel is accredited as the one to whom 'all authority in heaven and earth' has been given and whose commands are therefore to be taught and obeyed among all nations (28.16-20).

The claims to authority made for Moses and Jesus are in one sense analogous, inviting us to see them as comparable figures; in another sense they are rivalrous, precisely because of their scope. To say that 'all authority is given to me' is by implication to deny that others possess authority. Matthew wants to preserve his lines with the Jewish tradition; but he wants to be the judge of the nature of that continuity.

Perhaps this contrast between Jesus and Moses is most clearly indicated in the final clause of the Gospel: 'and lo, I am with you always, to the close of the age'. There are clear echoes here of two very important verses in the Gospel, 1.23 and 18.20. Whereas Moses was brought into the presence of God at significant points of his life, see, for example, Exodus 3 and 18 and the people of Israel are accompanied by the pillar of fire, Jesus is himself the presence of God with his people. Moreover he will be with them wherever they gather to pray. Matthew's retention of the incident of the tearing of the veil of the Temple strongly suggests that the presence of God which was previously associated with the Temple has now passed to Jesus himself, however paradoxical this may appear in view of Jesus' death.

Thus in the end Matthew is pointing clearly enough to the way in which Jesus transcends Moses and the old dispensation. It is evidently important to him to stress the continuity between God's purposes in the old dispensation and what is now taking place, as the 'fulfilment quotations' show. Similarly, it is important for him to show that there is consistency between God's revelation of his will in the Mosaic legislation and Jesus' own teaching. But here there is an equally strong concern to assert that Jesus' teaching transcends that of the old legislation; that true authority now lies with the Christian community which has indeed received the divine commission to propagate Jesus' commandments throughout the world.

Matthew's Christology as Narrative Christology

Allison's study is principally a study of allusion, of the rhetorical device of comparison, though of course it attends, within this overall aim, to narrative structures and circumstance. Fuller attention to the christological import of Matthew's *narrative* is given by Ulrich Luz in an important article: 'A Sketch of Matthew's Christology in the Form of Theses'.

Ulrich Luz has certainly produced some of the most elegant and carefully researched work on Matthew in the last fifteen years. As yet he has not produced a full statement of his views on Matthew's christology in his commentary, but in a number of articles he has begun to set them out. In the article just mentioned he is principally concerned with Matthew's use of three titles: Son of David, Son of Man and Son of God. He considers them, however, within the narrative of the Gospel, which he believes determines their meaning. For whereas before the Gospels it was the titles which served to say who Jesus was (which, as he puts it, were used 'predicatively'), in Matthew it is the other way round: 'the Matthaean story of Jesus functions as the predicate and redefines the meaning of the traditional titles' ('Sketch', p. 223). In this sense the meaning of the traditional titles becomes fluid.

Matthew's story is an inclusive story: it tells the story of Jesus' life in such a way that the whole history of his mission to Israel, of the divisions which it provokes, his judgment by the leaders of the Jewish people and his sending of the disciples to the nations, mirrors that of the church. 'It is the story of the "Emmanuel" (1.23, cf. 28.20), Jesus, which tells how in Jesus "God is with us", that is to say how Jesus accompanies his community along their way through obedience, experience of faith and suffering' (p. 223). The Emmanuel formula with its deep Old Testament roots, shows how far the christology of the Gospel is theology. 'Jesus in Matthew's Gospel is the new and definitive form of God's presence with his people' (p. 223).

What then of the three titles? 'Son of David' indicates that Jesus comes as the expected Messiah—but in practice he acts very differently to what is expected of him. Above all he heals, something not traditionally associated with the Son of David; Luz thinks that Matthew's inspiration for the interpretation of the title comes from Mark, esp. 10.46-52. In particular he heals the blind (9.27; 12.22; 20.30-31, cf. 21.14-16). 'The Messiah Jesus heals (metaphorically) the blindness of Israel, while the leaders remain blind (cf. 23.16-26)' (p. 225) However, 22.1-46 shows that the Son of David is more than Messiah, he is the Lord of the world and in the main christological sections of the last chapters the title no longer appears. Its purpose was to 'characterize Jesus' coming as the fulfilment and transformation of Israel's hopes and so to help overcome the shock of the separation of Christian congregation and synagogue' (p. 226).

More significant in the end are the two other titles. 'Son of Man' is again a title which Matthew takes over from the tradition. Matthew assumes that his readers know that the Son of Man is homeless and rejected, that he must suffer and die and that he will come to judge the world. It is a title that is to say which reminds the reader of the whole course of Jesus' story and which Matthew uses carefully. Luz differs, however, from Kingsbury in his assessment of the way Matthew uses it. He agrees that before 16.13 the majority of the Son of Man sayings are directed to the public. But thereafter Jesus speaks only to the disciples of the Son of Man with the exception of 26.64. In fact with two exceptions Jesus never speaks publicly about the Son of Man as coming judge or as the one who will suffer and rise again. It is only the sayings about the present Son of Man that are addressed to the public and these occur predominantly in the first half of the Gospel. Luz agrees with Kingsbury that the phrase is not used predicatively; it is not, that is to say, 'used to say who Jesus is, but to narrate what he does or suffers' (p. 227). In his reworking of the traditional material which he has taken over, Matthew has emphasised above all the sayings about the future coming of the Son of Man as judge (new sayings at 13.41; 16.28; 19.28?; 24.30a; 25.31).

How then does Matthew use the term in his Gospel? It is above all a phrase which draws a line between those who understand who Jesus is and those who do not, between the disciples and the 'ignorant and evil intentioned opponents on whom the judgment of the Son of Man will suddenly and unexpectedly fall' (p. 228). Thus Luz can speak of a 'Son of Man secret' in Matthew's Gospel. Just as the disciples in Mark are not to reveal the secret of Jesus' identity as the Messiah, so in Matthew the secret of his identity as Son of Man is hidden from those outside the community of the church, though in this case it is only rarely reinforced by a command to silence (16.20; 17.9). Above all, the title functions to hold together the various aspects of Jesus' life, including his future coming as judge. It is 'a horizontal title', which by contrast with the 'Son of David' title has a universal and future perspective.

Luz is fully aware of the questions about the origins of christology with which we started. His treatment is designed to address such questions. For him Matthew's 'horizontal' Son of Man christology forms a bridge between Jewish apocalyptic expectation of a heavenly cosmic judge and the later two natures christology which used the expression Son of Man for the humanity of Jesus. In such developments Matthew is taking up tendencies already present in Mark, particularly in his second part (8.31–14.62) which as we noted he follows more closely than the first. But he also 'deepens and reinforces Mark's horizontal understanding of the Son of Man with the help of the paradoxical use of the expression in Q (e.g. Q 9.58 the homeless Jesus as judge of the world)' (p. 231). From here the lines lead on to the use of the term in Ignatius of Antioch (early second century).

How then does this relate to the 'Son of God' title in Matthew? Matthew takes over the title from Mark where it

has a strongly vertical sense (and where it also has a confessional sense) and adds to it a horizontal dimension which
stresses Jesus' obedience to the Father. Here he is developing elements already to be found in Mark (willing acceptance of suffering) and Q (temptation stories) but is also
drawing importantly on the Jewish notion of the righteous
man who suffers unjustly (Ps. 22; Wis. 2.18).

Luz agrees with Kingsbury that Matthew places important
Son of God passages at the climaxes of the main sections of
his Gospel (though he disagrees with Kingsbury's threefold
division, seeing 11.25-30 as forming the climax of the second
section of the Gospel which runs from 4.23–11.30) and he
shows how in practically all important Son of God texts the
vertical and horizontal dimensions are combined. 11.25-30 in
particular shows how Matthew combines an interest in the
ethical dimension (not least through his addition of a
Wisdom saying, vv. 28-30 with its emphasis on Jesus' obedience: 'gentle and lowly in heart') of Jesus' existence with a
high christology which stresses 'the mutual "mystical" knowledge' of the Father and the Son (p. 233). The central
fulfilment quotation of 12.18-21 speaks not of the Servant of
God, as David Hill argues, but 'uses the biblical language of
Isaiah to speak of the *child* of God, that is, the Son of God
who is known to the readers from 3.17' (p. 233). But while
the Son of God title marks out major junctures of the Gospel
it does not appear in the final section 28.16-20 (except in the
triadic baptismal formula) though there are echoes of other
important christological passages. 'In this way it shows the
way in which Matthew's narrated christology is greater than
the titles which he uses. Matthaean christology is more than
a semantic field which is determined by titles which define
different aspects of the field; it is the story of a man in whom
God is and was "with us" ' (p. 234).

Conclusion

Matthew, we have seen, develops his views about Jesus'
person and relationship to God by weaving titles and motifs
from his tradition into a rich narrative. Focusing on the titles
is one way to see what Matthew is attempting, but it needs
at the least to be supplemented by a consideration of the

narrative setting of the titles and their interaction with other motifs. This means, I think, that we cannot expect to extract a neatly formulable christology from the Gospel. We can see how certain emphases are being set: clearly on the close relation of Jesus to his Father and his purposes. He is the one declared by the Father as his Son who is obedient to him and to whom all authority will be entrusted. He is the one who fulfils, but strangely, the hopes of Israel and thus can be seen in a sense as Son of David, as a new Moses, as mirroring in his own history the key moments of the history of Israel, above all as announcing the will of God to his people. But the fact is that Matthew sets all this in the context of a story which relates Jesus' humiliation and death as well as his resurrection from the dead. In simple terms Jesus touches depths and heights which are not attained by the figures from the past with whom Jesus is most closely associated— David, Elijah, Moses. And the claim is that God does not simply use this strange figure as his messenger and instrument, but that he is in his very lowliness, obedience and suffering, as well as in his exaltation, God with us.

As Luz has suggested it is possible to see a line of development between Matthew's christology with its equal emphases on Jesus' Sonship and his earthly fate as Son of Man and the later thought of the church which used the terminology of Son of God and Son of Man to develop a doctrine of the two natures, the divinity and the humanity of Christ. If one of the features of earliest Christian belief in Christ was belief in his coming as the heavenly judge at the end of time, then here the narration of his life and death is the means whereby reflection can begin to encompass the meaning of his earthly life and suffering. It too shares, more or less evidently, in the authority which will be manifested in the final judgment.

Thus Matthew has created a rich subject for subsequent Christian thought and reflection. The two natures christology of the early Church is of course only one way in which it could be developed. Christian theology will constantly have to struggle to find ways of expressing the mystery of the presence of God in the figure of the suffering, crucifed and risen Christ to which Matthew has given such powerful expression.

Matthew

Further Reading

D.C. Allison, Jr, 'The Son of God as Israel: A Note on Matthean Christology', *Irish Biblical Studies* 9 (1987), pp. 74-81.

—*The New Moses: A Matthean Typology* (Minneapolis: Fortress Press, 1993).

R.E. Brown, *The Birth of the Messiah* (New York: Doubleday, 1977).

D. Hill, 'Son and Servant: An Essay on Matthean Christology', *JSNT* 6 (1980), pp. 2-16.

J.D. Kingsbury, *Matthew: Structure, Christology, Kingdom* (Minneapolis: Fortress Press, 2nd edn, 1989 [1975]).

—*Matthew as Story* (Philadelphia: Fortress Press, 1986).

—'The Figure of Jesus in Matthew's Story: a Literary-Critical Probe', *JSNT* 21 (1984), pp. 3-36.

—'The Figure of Jesus in Matthew's Story: A Rejoinder to David Hill', *JSNT* 25 (1985), pp. 61-81.

U. Luz, 'A Sketch of Matthew's Christology in the Form of Theses', available only in German as 'Eine thetische Skizze der matthäischen Christologie', in C. Breytenbach and H. Paulsen (eds.), *Anfänge der Christologie* (Göttingen: Vandenhoeck & Ruprecht, 1991), pp. 221-35.

W. Wrede, *The Messianic Secret* (Cambridge: James Clarke, 1971) (first published in German in 1901).

5

CONCLUSION

Matthew's Gospel is a work of contrasts: it takes Mark's rough and dramatic narrative and inserts into it large blocks of teaching material which might well seem to threaten its narrative force, turning it into a mere teaching manual for the church. But this does not happen: the narrative, though undoubtedly flattened in some places, continues to draw the reader into the story of Jesus and his disciples. As it does so, it provides further grounds for reflection on the complex figure of this teacher, healer, Lord and redeemer, reflection focused partly on the titles given to him, partly on the rich allusions to Israel's past which his story contains and partly by the conjunction of all this with the narrative of his life, death and resurrection.

It is then scarcely surprising that this diverse and complex book has provided a steady source of inspiration for church leaders, theologians, legislators, preachers and believers through the centuries, so much so that for long it largely overshadowed its darker and more dramatic forebear, Mark. That is to say, it is in an important sense a perennial Gospel. It is a primary source of theological reflection on the nature of Jesus' sonship; it embeds the Christian story firmly into the traditions of Israel and the Hebrew Scriptures; it sets out the teaching of Jesus in its fullest and most systematic form.

All of this might seem to argue for a treatment of Matthew's Gospel which is less rather than more historical: the circumstances of its genesis might well be thought to be less significant than its perennially fruitful contents, however achieved. And yet we have spent—and scholarly

studies of Matthew still spend—much time on relating the
Gospel to the community in and for which it was written. Is
this simple academic perversity, the habits of the guild,
which should have been long since abandoned? I think not:
for the history can help to shed light on the strange and
fruitful contrasts which typify the book.

Matthew's Gospel, it has been argued, is in important
senses sectarian: it is the work of a writer seeking to
strengthen his community, to enable it to assert its own distinctive identity over against the more powerful (if trauma-
tized) Jewish community in which it has its roots. But it does
not just see itself as a 'new people' to whom the Kingdom has
now been entrusted (21.43); it also sees itself as living out
the fulfilment of all that has been promised of old. Just at the
moment of the sharpest sense of rupture with the past
Matthew vigorously asserts his community's continuity with
that past. It is Matthew (and to a lesser extent Luke) more
than Mark, John or indeed Paul (Galatians!) who ties
Christianity to the traditions of Israel and ensures that the
Christian Bible is composed of two 'testaments'; just as it is
Matthew who ensures that this relationship will be a stormy
and indeed tragic one.

The Matthaean community's separation from Judaism
leaves its marks in other ways. In his sense of separateness
from the mainstream of society, Matthew sets out, foremost
in the Sermon on the Mount, the guidelines for a new way of
life. It is an alternative community ethic, in significant ways
sharply contrasted with the dominant ethos of the surrounding culture (antitheses; ch. 23!). This radical ethic has posed
problems for the church when it has itself entered into the
mainstream of political and cultural life and found it increasingly difficult *not* to compromise the bright ('utopian'?) ideals
of the Sermon on the Mount. By the same token it can
provide a source of inspiration for those who find themselves
out of sorts with their contemporary culture and who seek
renewal and reinvigoration.

One thing is sure: interest in Matthew is unlikely to dimin-
ish. Where Matthaean studies will be in ten years time, I will
not speculate. Let me finally suggest two areas where it
would be timely for there to be further work. First, Luz's

work on the history of interpretation whets the appetite for more, this is surely one area where much illumination is to be gained; and secondly, there is room for more thought to be given to the place of Matthew's theology within the theologies of early Christianity. How does Matthew's theology relate to Paul's—and also to Mark's and John's and Luke's? Comparative studies would help to throw all those compared into a sharper light.

Recommendations for Further Reading

As will be clear I have been most helped and have drawn most on the works of two scholars.

G. Stanton, *A Gospel for a New People: Studies in Matthew* (Edinburgh: T. & T. Clark, 1992). This is an attractively written book which engages with both social-historical and literary-critical questions in a fresh and persuasive way. For those who would like something briefer from the same author, *The Gospels and Jesus* (Oxford: Oxford University Press, 1989) is a useful introduction to Gospel study; *The Interpretation of Matthew* (London: SPCK, 1983) provides a selection of important articles in the field of Matthaean studies, with a helpful introduction.

U. Luz, *Matthew 1–7* (Minneapolis: Fortress Press, 1989 [vol. 2 presently only available in German]) is in some ways a fairly traditional commentary, paying close attention to Matthew's editing of his sources and basing its findings on a close reconstruction of the traditions behind Matthew. But he is a master of this craft and shows its strengths, not least because he is aware of its difficulties. The real discovery of the commentary is the light it sheds on the Gospel through the history of effects. For those who want to follow this up Luz's *Matthew in History: Interpretation, Influence, and Effects* (Minneapolis: Fortress Press, 1994) contains some valuable essays. For those who want more detailed work on the Jewish background to the Gospel, W.D. Davies and D.C. Allison, Jr, *A Critical and Exegetical Commentary on the Gospel according to Matthew* (Edinburgh: T. & T. Clark, 1988, 1991) provides a rich store. For handier and cheaper commentaries, D. Hill, *The Gospel of Matthew* (London: Oliphants, 1972) and E. Schweizer, *The Good News According to Matthew* (London: SPCK, 1976) are generally reliable and informative. For those who would like to explore literary approaches to the Gospel, there is R.H. Gundry, *Matthew: A Commentary on his Literary and Theological Art* (Grand Rapids: Eerdmans, 1982).

There are, of course, many other works which I have drawn on, some of which are contained in the lists at the end of each chapter.

These too can be explored and will lead the reader to more and more books and articles. The important thing is not to be overwhelmed by the flood of literature: it is there for you to use and to guide you in your own lines of enquiry.

INDEXES

INDEX OF REFERENCES

INDEX OF AUTHORS